LAUREL

MARGARET MEAD   JAMES BALDWIN
A RAP ON RACE

"THE ONLY PUBLISHED 'CONFRONTATION' OF ITS KIND."
—*The New York Times*

"A COGENT, SEARCHING INQUIRY INTO HUMAN EXISTENCE. Dr. Mead brings to the dialogue the rich insights of her massive tradition of scholarship which has contributed so importantly to our knowledge of other peoples and of ourselves. Novelist and essayist Baldwin tunes in with a fine intellect and his singular ability to interpret and generalize his own black experience."
—*Boston Sunday Globe*

"BALDWIN IS SO GIFTED AND EVEN OVERWHELMING A TALKER, MONOLOGIST, PREACHER—no one around practices the old-fashioned art of spellbinding with such force— that he manages, astonishingly, to slip past Margaret Mead's friendly but obstinate questioning of his emotional position."
—Alfred Kazin, *Saturday Review*

"FASCINATING, INTELLIGENT, KNOWLEDGEABLE, SENSITIVE, CONCERNED. . . . There are moments of poetry, of anger, of humor. All kinds of sparks."
—*The Charlotte Observer*

"A PERTINENT, ILLUMINATING AND RICHLY HUMAN CONVERSATION. Seldom in book form has there been an exchange between two such informed, civilized and mutually respectful—but passionately honest—citizens of the mind as this one."
—*Publishers Weekly*

A RAP ON RACE

James Baldwin........

....Margaret Mead

LAUREL

A LAUREL BOOK
Published by
Dell Publishing
a division of
Bantam Doubleday Dell Publishing Group, Inc.
666 Fifth Avenue
New York, New York 10103

The trademark Laurel® is registered in the U.S. Patent and Trademark Office.

The trademark Dell® is registered in the U.S. Patent and Trademark Office.

ISBN: 0-440-21176-X

Reprinted by arrangement with J. B. Lippincott

Printed in the United States of America

Published simultaneously in Canada

February 1992

10 9 8 7 6 5 4 3 2 1

RAD

Editor's Note

Margaret Mead and James Baldwin met for the first time on the evening of August 25, 1970. They spent approximately one hour getting acquainted. On the following evening they sat down to discuss race and society. Their discussion was resumed the next morning and again that night. The entire conversation lasted approximately seven and one half hours. It was tape-recorded, and this book, *A Rap on Race*, is the transcript made from those tapes.

August 26th...8 P.M.

BALDWIN: Everyone really knows how long the blacks have been here. Everyone knows on what level blacks are involved with the American people and in American life. These are not secrets. It is not a question even of the ignorance of white people. It is a question of the fears of white people.

MEAD: Yes, I know.

BALDWIN: So that's what makes it all so hysterical, so unwieldy and so completely irretrievable. Reason cannot reach it. It is as though some great, great, great wound is in the whole body, and no one dares to operate: to close it, to examine it, to stitch it.

MEAD: You know, one thing I've been interested in, in reading your work, is when you talked about America as so unique and, of course, when you say there are no "Negroes" outside of America. I know exactly what you mean. That's true. But you never talk about South Africa.

BALDWIN: I never talk about South Africa because I don't know anything about the South African society, really. I've never been to South Africa. I've met some South Africans, some of whom I liked and some of whom I didn't.

MEAD: But, you know, one of the curious things is that I've heard in the voices of white South Africans, when they say "my country," the same kinds of things I hear in your voice when you say "I'm an American."

BALDWIN: Oh, that makes sense, too. Although the sense it makes is rather hideous. But I can understand that, because after all the white South Africans are a minority in South Africa.

MEAD: And they have no other home.

BALDWIN: They're down there at the very end of the earth with nothing but the sea before them. If—it's not *if*, when —the holocaust comes there'll be nobody to help them.

MEAD: That's right. They've cut themselves off.

BALDWIN: They've cut themselves off completely. It is one of the most tragic things in the world, one of the most tragic groups of people in the world, because there is no hope for them. And when they say "It is my country," I think I know what they mean. They mean that they were born there; they mean that they suffered and died for the land—very much like white Southerners. And as deluded as white Southerners, because now they've painted themselves into a corner. They are in an absolutely hostile continent. In their own country they are surrounded and outnumbered by black people. And the white South African regime, which might last perhaps ten—at most another twenty-five—years, is obviously doomed. The whole way of life, a whole way of life, is doomed.

Which means that somewhere—this is what I'd like to get at—somewhere, something happened to white people one day, I don't know what it was, which dictated their sense of reality. It has something to do with their apprehension of religion, whatever indeed that is. But it's a very complex matter.

MEAD: I recall a boy whose father married again, married a woman who had a son about the same age. They weren't related, of course; they were stepbrothers. And then that father and mother, the father of the first boy and the mother of the second, had a child. And the first boy said, "Now I feel differently about it. We have a brother in common."

BALDWIN: Ah, that makes a great deal of difference.

MEAD: You see, this is true in a sense. Because as far as I know—and this is all any white person of the United States can ever say—as far as I know, I haven't any black ancestry. But you've got some white ancestry.

BALDWIN: Yes, yes.

MEAD: So we've got a brother in common.

BALDWIN: So we've got a brother in common. But isn't the tragedy partly related to the fact that most white people deny their brother?

MEAD: Well, there are two kinds of tragedy, and I think that's one of the things we have to get clear. There is a tragedy of denying brotherhood when there is an ancestral tie that is at least ten thousand years away or maybe one hundred thousand years away. I mean, my relationship to someone in New Guinea and your relationship to someone in New Guinea is thousands of years away, although we're all human beings and we all belong to one species. That's one kind of brotherhood. The other kind of brotherhood is where people have been so close that they are really related in the sense that one talks about blood relationships.

BALDWIN: That's what I mean in the case of the black American who is called a black or Negro.

MEAD: That's the thing in this country, you see. But in this country the relationship is so close.

BALDWIN: That's right.

MEAD: And it's another kind.

BALDWIN: Well, I wonder. Perhaps it's a very bizarre wonder, but I can't quite get myself into the head of, let us say—we're speaking in such horrible generalities, speaking of white people or black people—but I can't think myself into the head of a white man, let us say, who knows very well that he has a son or a daughter or a brother who is legally black. He knows it—it isn't something that he doesn't know—and he pretends that it isn't so.

MEAD: In the South they didn't use to pretend it wasn't so.

BALDWIN: Everybody knew it.

MEAD: You know, something happened a couple of years ago in the South that I was very interested in. In Georgia, they elected the first black woman—among the first black legislators in fifty years—to the state legislature. She is Grace Towns Hamilton, great-grandniece of former Governor Towns of the state.

And her father, George Towns, taught in Atlanta University. So, as a young woman she was known by her maiden name—Grace Towns. She's very tall, long-limbed, with a sort of upper-class Englishwoman's style.

And the day she entered the legislature, where her ancestor's portrait hangs, she collected the little black page boys—this was a first for them too—and went and stood under her ancestor's portrait and had her picture taken. That was all she did. She claimed him. Now, at that point I thought—I heard this story just about the time that "black is beautiful" was coming up—all the change in the way black people were thinking about integration; all these things were coming up—and I thought that one of the things that's got to be done in this country is all the black people have got to claim their white ancestors. Everybody's got to claim all their ancestors and all their cousins. That's one thing. Then the other thing, of course, is that in this country people have always adopted ancestors they haven't any business to.

BALDWIN: Exactly.

MEAD: Of course, George Washington didn't have any children, fortunately. And so we have always been able to make up our ancestors and go around and take other people's. Now, I remember a conversation with a friend of mine years ago, named Rachel Davis DuBois. Did you ever encounter her? She's a Quaker, and she's made up a thing called a community festival where a mixed group of people sit around telling about things that happened and singing songs. She's got a lot of quality.

Anyway, she was talking about someone being angry because someone else had taken their name. I mean, their name was say Smith and they went and took the name of Sturtevant or Livingston or something of that sort. And I was objecting to the attitudes of the Sturtevants who were objecting to them taking their name and she turned around to me and said, "Would you take Crispus Attucks for your ancestor?"

At that point I thought, Why? Why do I have to take him as my ancestor, because he isn't my ancestor? True, George Washington wasn't anybody's ancestor either; he was only a mythical ancestor, too. But I didn't see why I should take the first black man killed in the American Revolution as my ancestor. This was in the midst of the fight for integration, when everybody was very generously saying to black people—that is, the white people who believed in integration—"We'll share what we have with you." And they thought that was all the generosity that was needed, you see. So in those terms I had some nice white ancestors to share with you. That's all I needed.

BALDWIN: Yes, yes.

MEAD: And I didn't feel that I needed for you to share any black ancestors with me. But we know now that I do. We didn't know then. This was, I suppose, twenty-five years ago when she said this to me. It is the key to the integration problem. I was speaking in those days about three things we had to do: appreciate cultural differences, respect political and religious differences and ignore race. Absolutely ignore race.

BALDWIN: Ignore race. That certainly seemed perfectly sound and true.

MEAD: Yes, but it isn't anymore. You see, it really isn't true. This was wrong, because—

BALDWIN: Because race cannot be ignored.

MEAD: Skin color can't be ignored. It is real. When we said ignore race . . . and I was so proud—you know, we were all proud whenever we forgot it.

BALDWIN: Yes.

MEAD: Even when we were in Washington, D.C., during the war and, if you forgot it, you were likely to get into trouble and embarrass somebody in a restaurant. Just the same, I remember I was bringing a group together and we were meeting in the Chamber of Commerce building, because I couldn't get a room that day at the Academy of Science. It suddenly struck me: Good God! One of the people coming in from New York was a Negro, and I didn't know what the Chamber of Commerce thought about this and I wasn't about to ask them. So I called up a Catholic priest who worked with my committee and asked him to come in full regalia. Then I called up a white member of the same group in New York and said, "Would you please come together?" And we never found out what the Chamber of Commerce felt. But I was very proud that I hadn't remembered.

BALDWIN: That you'd thought of it?

MEAD: No, I was proud that I hadn't remembered initially. It hadn't occurred to me at all.

BALDWIN: But, of course. That's what I mean when I say . . . when I hear "Ignore race." Well, it took me a long time to do that, and perhaps I would never have been able to do it if I hadn't left America. I *know* I wouldn't have been able to do it if I hadn't left America. It was a great revelation for me when I found myself finally in France among all kinds of very different people—I mean, at least different from anybody I had met in America. And I realized one day that somebody asked me about a friend of mine who, in fact, when I thought about it, is probably North African, but I really did not remember whether he was white or black. It simply had never occurred to me. The question had never been in my mind. Never in my mind.

I really had a terrible time. I suddenly felt as though I were lost. My whole frame of reference all the years I was growing up had been black and white. You know, you always knew who was white and who was black. But suddenly I didn't have it; suddenly that frame of reference had gone. And in a funny way—and I don't know how to make sense of this—as far as I could tell, as far as I can tell till this hour, once that has happened to you, it never comes back.

MEAD: I had to make it come back.

BALDWIN: Well, I came home.

MEAD: Well, I had to move from advocating integration only to the meaning of black power.

BALDWIN: I've had to do that, too. For very different reasons, perhaps, or probably the same reasons. But it doesn't affect my judgment of other people. You see, I know my situation is not the same situation I was in when Martin Luther King was alive and when we were trying, when we hoped to bring about some kind of revolution in the American conscience, which is, after all, where everything in some sense has to begin. Of course, that's gone now. It's gone because the Republic never had the courage or the ability or whatever it was that was needed to apprehend the nature of Martin's dream. Let me just put it that way; it is an oversimplification, but you know what I mean.

MEAD: Yes.

BALDWIN: So we're in another situation. We're in a very dangerous and complex situation, because part of. . . .

You know, your story of the great-grandniece of the Governor of Georgia is very revealing and very touching, but the reason that most black people will not do that is because we've been so humiliated for so long by all the white assumptions. And the vast amount, for example, of the energy which we call, misnamed in some sense, the "black power movement" is an *absolute* reaction, a reaction of real fury, because a whole generation is now growing up—is grown up—which is unlike my generation. This generation knows. It has seen it with its own eyes and has heard it with its own ears: the nature of the lies the white people told black people for generations. And it understands the reasons for these lies.

Whether or not they understand really what the situation is and what the future should be is not a question; it doesn't make any difference at the moment. What they are doing is repudiating the entire theology, as I call it, which has afflicted and destroyed—really, literally destroyed—black people in this country for so long. And what this generation is reacting to, what it is saying, is they realize that you, the white people, white Americans, have always attempted to murder them. Not merely by burning them or castrating them or hanging them from trees, but murdering them in the mind, in the heart.

By teaching a black child that he is worthless, that he can never contribute anything to civilization, you're teaching him how to hate his mother, his father, and his brothers. Everyone in my generation has seen the wreckage that this has caused. And what black kids are doing now, no matter how excessively, is right. They are refusing this entire frame of reference and they are saying to the Republic: This is your bill, this is your bloody bill written in my *blood,* and you are going to have to pay it.

MEAD: But don't you think, also, that it is not only the disillusionment of this younger generation, which I understand perfectly, but also it's a sensible position that you've got? That the integration position was a one-sided one?

BALDWIN: Yes, it was.

MEAD: And, of course, it was one that was shared in by both black and white. It was what, in a sense, many black people thought they wanted as individuals. They thought they wanted it, and then they had to learn that it was one-sided.

BALDWIN: Yes.

MEAD: That's what Fanon said when he wrote *Black Skin, White Masks*. But his point, that what the black man is offered as civilization is *white* civilization, deals more with French civilization than it does with American.

BALDWIN: It's clearer.

MEAD: It's much clearer. But, nevertheless, the offer— which is substantially the way I would phrase it—the offer that well-intentioned white people made is: "If you will be like us—

BALDWIN: "You could join our clubs and come to our houses—

MEAD: "And we'll pretend that you're just like us."

BALDWIN: Yeah.

MEAD: Which means of course that we'll deny you.

BALDWIN: Exactly.

MEAD: We'll deny your hair, we'll deny your skin, we'll deny your eyes. We deny you. We deny you when we accept you; we deny the ways in which you are not exactly us, by ignoring them.

BALDWIN: Yes.

MEAD: And what black power is saying is: I want to accept myself first, and my parents, and I want to enjoy the way my mother and father look, and from there—

BALDWIN: Then we'll see.

MEAD: Then we'll turn around. Then we'll see. You like the way your parents look, and—I mean if you're speaking to me now—

BALDWIN: Yeah, yeah.

MEAD: I like the way my parents look—most of the time.

When I'd lived in New Guinea too long or for a long time, I came back here and I didn't like babies being so huge and pale. I didn't mind other people, but I didn't like such white babies because I'd been holding all those thin little brown babies in my arms and they were so beautiful and our babies looked too fat and too big. They looked like whales and I didn't quite like it. And I don't much like the way white people look in the tropics because they get so sunburned and worn.

BALDWIN: Dried out.

MEAD: They weren't made for the tropics. The black people that are there look wonderful, and the white people look freckled and burned or deadly pale.

BALDWIN: Well, the sun is burning them out.

MEAD: It is burning them out. You know, it's not good for them. I look like a boiled beet if I go out in the tropical sun. But all the people in the world have got to be able to be proud of the way their parents look.

BALDWIN: Yes, without that they're lost.

MEAD: The looking is important. Now, when one said let's ignore race. . . . You see, now we'll ignore it. We had that long period when the Rosenwald Fund had been giving fellowships to young Negroes in the South. I went to a meeting in Chicago during World War II when the Rosenwald Fund called all the people in this country interested in race. Mary Bethune was there, and W.E.B. Du Bois. They had extraordinary heads and all sorts of diversity and character. But all the young men looked like Arrow-collar men. They looked much more like Arrow-collar men than the Arrow-collar ad looks like an ordinary group of white men. They were all picked out for just that sort of countenance.

I looked at that and said, "How we are sterotyping the

gifted young Negroes! In a sense, we're taking *our* ideal and we're picking Negro young men that look as close as possible to our ideal and giving them the opportunities; they get the scholarships." And, of course, this was being done inside the black family, too. Everybody was cooperating with this image.

BALDWIN: But those Black Arrow-collar men, as you put them, Arrow-collar-ad men, found themselves very quickly in serious psychological trouble, because they weren't, no matter how well the uniform fitted, really what they were taken to be or were hoping or pretending to be. They were not. And they went home after the meeting or—

MEAD: You could never tell where they went.

BALDWIN: They went into actually what for white people would be a kind of limbo. In any case, they returned, however they tried to avoid, it, to their real situation and found out they were alienated from the people who had produced them. And not only alienated in terms of having something in common or in terms of clothes or things like that, but in much more serious terms. They had lost their frame of reference. If I can't, for example, go home and get drunk with my brother or sit around with my brothers and sisters and just do nothing—you know, fry chicken or eat some watermelon or play some music—if I can't find myself with people who know enough about me to correct me, who are not intimidated by whatever it is the world thinks I am, or whatever I may think I am, if you don't find the people who know enough about you to do that and the people who love you enough to do that, then you are very quickly lost and you become a kind of walking cauldron.

Those Arrow-collar-ad men are very, very dangerous,

because really those people hate white people much more than the porter does. The porter hates you in quite an abstract way. But someone who thinks he is trying to be like you, and is always acting for you, and knows at bottom that really you despise him, is a candidate for a mental institution—where many of them end up, you know.

MEAD: Well, I think a few of them, when they now have to put on Afro hairdress, are really candidates for trouble.

BALDWIN: That's schizophrenia, you know.

MEAD: Then they are really candidates for trouble.

BALDWIN: Well, I am old enough to know an awful lot of people who spent most of their lives trying to be white. They wouldn't speak to me. They put everybody down. Nappy hair, funky music and Ray Charles—you know. They thought they were "together," and then somebody switched the signals on them. Like one very famous singer with conked hair, really a kind of travesty of all the popular singers you ever saw in America. All of a sudden the conked hair made him suspect and his friends looked upon him with great disfavor and he had to wash his hair and just let it be kinky and change his whole image overnight. He managed to do it; he's a very tough and cunning businessman. But a whole lot of other people simply got caught in the middle of the street when the traffic light shifted. A lot of them were brushed off the stage of history, as we would put it, never to be heard of again.

It's funny, but it's terrible. It says so much about what the real aims of this Republic have always been, what the real price a black person has paid for being able to live here at all, you know. And no one has really ever managed to record that price except in music or some weird, unexpected places like the Negro church. If you actually

try to take apart a black man's sermon and really understand what he is saying, it's kind of terrifying. But the
bulk of the Republic has somehow managed to go along
singing like Doris Day in the sun and the rain and has
never heard a word of it. And now what's happened is
that, for this moment in our history, anyway, black people
no longer care what white people think. I no longer care,
to tell you the truth, whether white people can hear me
or not. It doesn't make any difference at all. If they can
hear me, so much the better; if they can't, so much the
worse. For them.

MEAD: In a way, I can really understand this. When I'm in
New Guinea, when I'm living in a village completely related to everyone in the village, they're the people that
matter, and nobody else matters. I'm not particularly conscious any longer that I'm white, that I'm an anthropologist from a long way off, because there are too many other
things to be conscious of.

One year we had a house where we could see down to
the banks of the river. A boat would come up and the
boat would stop and people would get off. All around me
would be lots of New Guinea people: mothers with their
babies in their arms—whole groups of people. And white
men would get off that boat. I could see that they were
white before I knew who they were, because they wear
different kinds of clothes and they are much bigger and
so forth. The unknown white men would get off the boat,
and they looked to me like paper dolls. They didn't look
like real people at all. And as they came closer, and I
could see who they were and either recognize them or
not recognize them, they became individuals. And then
the people around me turned into paper dolls. You see,
the break was so great; the break was so great that you

couldn't look at both worlds at once. So one of them became unreal, two-dimensional, flat.

BALDWIN: That must be very, very strange. You know, I'm very curious about how long you were in New Guinea.

MEAD: Well, one time I was there for three years.

BALDWIN: I'm very curious about what you know about that. I have a feeling there is something in that, something which you know.

MEAD: The things I learned in New Guinea, after all, I learned late. I learned about race when I was a child.

BALDWIN: How did you learn about that?

MEAD: I lived on a farm that had been a station for the underground railroad.

BALDWIN: In the North, then.

MEAD: In the North, in Bucks County, Pennsylvania. I have completely Northern ancestry, and my grandfather fought in the Civil War on the Northern side. My father bought a farm that had been a station on the underground railroad. This history we regarded as very good, romantic, good Northern behavior. And we had two old Negro men in the neighborhood—we called them *colored* then, in 1912 —who had been slaves but who dropped off and hid and stayed behind. One of them had a younger wife—he must have been seventy, I suppose, when I was a child, but he had a younger wife—a very fat, very black wife. She had a half-white son, and what I was told by my mother—who believed in telling children the truth and telling it correctly so they wouldn't get it wrong—was that she'd been raped by a white man. You see, I had the reverse picture that most Americans have, because most white women picture a rapist as a black man. This is one of the important things one has to remember all the time.

BALDWIN: This is very funny. Go on.

MEAD: But I had reversed it, and my picture of rape was of a black woman raped by a white man. He was a butcher, too, and that's one of the things I thought of: he was a brutal character. So whenever I dreamt of rape, I dreamt of this black woman being raped by a white man. And our mother insisted on our calling her *Mrs.*—this is 1912. And whenever she turned up in a dream, I knew exactly what I was dreaming about. This is a straight reversal of ordinary American experience.

BALDWIN: That's right. The ordinary American mythology is entirely different. I suppose that explains a lot about you.

MEAD: Probably, although I'm not completely free. You see, I don't think any American—any white American—is free of a special attitude toward American Negroes. Just as you're saying there aren't any Negroes outside of America. We are often nice to other dark-skinned peoples. We treat African princes or Indians with turbans very well. When I went on. . . . My first field trip was to Samoa. Well, of course, the Polynesians are people everybody thinks are beautiful. If you look at them very closely, they are not really the most beautiful people in the world by any absolute standard. Yet everybody thinks they're beautiful. Chinese people think so, black people think so, everybody thinks so. I've now figured out why: that for maybe two or three thousand years they never saw anybody but themselves, and *they* think they're beautiful and they are so impressed with themselves that everybody else thinks they're beautiful. If you think you're beautiful, you move like a beautiful person.

BALDWIN: In a certain way, yes, that's right.

MEAD: They said, "She's the prettiest girl in the village," and "she's the ugliest." They made gradations, of course. And they were the first people I went and worked

among. I slept on their beds and went fishing with them
and dancing with them. I was much smaller than they
were, so I could work with adolescent girls and act as if I
was a fourteen-year-old when really I was twenty-three
years old. But then I remember I was surprised when I
went back just before I left, to the village that I had
stayed at in the beginning, and of course by this time I
spoke the language fluently. One of the girls said to me,
"We watched you when you came. We watched you and
we saw what you did. I offered to lend you a comb and
you took it. We watched." But I hadn't been conscious at
all.

Then I went to New Guinea. You know, these are your
very, very faraway cousins; they are mostly yours yet also
they are mine, from thousands of centuries back. They
have black skins and they have magnificent hair that you
can comb straight up into the air and cut patterns on. And
among one of the people I studied, Arapesh, there was
just one of the teenage boys I knew very well who looked
a little bit more like an American Negro. Just a little
more, just a touch more, and I always had a slight aware-
ness, you know. I was holding their babies in my arms,
and nursing them when they were sick, and they were
carrying me around, and everything. Yet with this one boy
I would notice in myself just a touch of self-consciousness. That's all it was, but it was self-consciousness.

BALDWIN: But there it was. Yes, I know what you mean.

MEAD: And it was still there.

BALDWIN: Yes.

MEAD: In spite of the reversals. I grew up with a positive
    premium on people who had no race prejudice. My
    grandmother gave me lectures on how the mother of our
    Lord was a Jew. So I went out and collected Jewish chil-

dren, liked them very much, had a lot of friends who were Jewish. It was very positive, my upbringing, so I was all prepared for working on integration at any possible level.

BALDWIN: But what I'm curious about: You say that no white American can avoid having a special attitude?

MEAD: And no black American.

BALDWIN: Okay, and no black American. But before we get to that, what do you think out of your own experience is this special attitude that white Americans have toward black Americans? It's composed of what?

MEAD: Consciousness first, I'd say. It's part of the things you notice.

BALDWIN: Of the difference?

MEAD: Well, consciousness that there are different kinds of people and you've got to remember it. I think that this is the point.

BALDWIN: Yes, but it depends on—

MEAD: That you've *got* to remember it.

BALDWIN: The question is why *do* you have to remember it? Well, I mean, the question for me.

MEAD: Now this is what I would answer. It's a way of life that I've lived in that's so far back in your people's experience that you can't tap your memories anymore because there aren't even any old people in this country alive who can give it to you.

But you see, I've been on a plantation in New Guinea where I was responsible for a labor line. Now, they weren't slaves. They were indentured laborers; they were grown men. You have two hundred men out of the bush. Some of them had been cannibals. Some of them weren't cannibals; some of them had just been good, fiery fighters. But they came out of a very, very primitive technical society. New Guinea is a very primitive society; it isn't like

Africa. You do have some people in Africa as primitive as people in New Guinea, but New Guinea had no kingdoms and no great traditions at all. They couldn't hold more than five hundred people together politically.

Now, when I was temporarily alone, I had to run that labor line. I had to give them orders based on absolutely nothing but white supremacy. I was one lone white woman. Any one of them could have killed me, and it was my business not to get killed. If anything had happened to me, maybe twenty of *them* would have been killed.

I've also been alone in a village where there wasn't a single white person within two days' walk. All alone and nothing but women in the village. All the men had gone away and some strange men came into the village and came to my house and sat down and wanted to sell me some poor beans. Now if I took the worm-eaten beans I was in danger, so I had to refuse the worm-eaten beans. I said, "No, they're no good. I won't buy them." So they walked out of the house, and when they were gone the box of matches was gone off the table.

I had to get that box of matches back. If I didn't, I would have been as good as dead. White people who let a thief go used to be killed; they had shown themselves as weak. So I stormed up to the end of the village. This was a fine exercise of sheer white supremacy, nothing else. I didn't have another thing. I didn't have a gun. I walked up to the end of the village and they were all sitting around in a circle and I said, "Give me those matches back." And one man put his hand in his bag and said, "I didn't steal them; I just took them," and handed them back. Then we were all safe. Now if I had made one misstep I'd have been dead, and then the administration would have sent in a punitive expedition and they would have been dead.

This is the burden, in a sense, that in this country the black man and the white woman carried in plantation days. If a white woman made a mistake, or didn't remember who she was every single second, everyone would suffer. So you never forget you must never turn your back, never let anybody steal from you, keep your nerve. You have nothing but nerve to protect you. I lock up the guns when I am alone.

This is what we've had in the South. I'd read all the books, but I'd never gone south until 1942; and when I crossed the Mason-Dixon line I felt I was not in the United States, I was in New Guinea. Because this kind of thing isn't true in the North. It may crop up, but it isn't a Northern feeling, that you have to be aware of what you do every minute, every single minute. I've carried this burden to the point where it meant life and death every second. You think of those early days in the South, and the strongest men were the only ones that survived. Everybody else had died in the slave ships.

BALDWIN: Yes, that's true.

MEAD: So they were the strongest people and, on a plantation twenty miles from anywhere, left in charge of a white woman very often. And she carried everybody's lives in her hands and so did the strongest of the black men. They had to keep things steady.

BALDWIN: It's a devastating relationship, you know.

MEAD: All desperate relationships are devastating. I used to do a lot of lecturing on race in the 1940s, and I had some rules. People had to stand on their two feet to ask questions. To ask me if I wanted my daughter to marry a Negro, they were going to stand up and look me in the eye. And my answer was, "Yes, if she respects him and he respects her."

BALDWIN: Yes.

MEAD: "But," I added, "I think at the present moment that every marriage in Nazi Germany is a very bad marriage, because men don't respect women, and I don't think that any marriage is good unless both partners respect each other."

BALDWIN: That's it, of course.

MEAD: Now when you have any terrific disparity in power it produces terrible relationships.

BALDWIN: Yes. Of course, at the root of all this is power, isn't it?

MEAD: Power and fear.

BALDWIN: Which has become pathological. I went south very late, too. I went south for the first time, I guess, in 1957. I'd never been south before. Now I had, before that. . . . This was, I guess, my first real encounter with Southern racial terrors, because growing up in Harlem you know very soon why you're there and the white people feel very strange for you and it isn't true in the beginning that you hate them. It's just that you don't know who they are.

MEAD: You don't know who they are and you don't go near them.

BALDWIN: You don't go near them, but you feel menaced by them. All kinds of things happen in Harlem, but Harlem is a colored community. You know, everyone around me was colored. So the white thing didn't really break in completely. What really must have happened, I can see now, is that I blotted a lot of it out, out of pure panic. Because a kid doesn't know how to handle it, really.

My teachers were white, most of them. I didn't like

most of them, but it wasn't because they were white that I didn't like them. It was just because they were strange. My favorite teacher happened to be a black lady; then, later on, a white school teacher who was a Communist. In those years everybody had to be a Communist, really, obviously, you know. If I had been three years older, I would have been a Communist, too. But she fed us and took me to the theater and things like that. And she was the first human being to sort of move out of that kind of monolithic mass that is composed of the landlords, the pawnbrokers and the cops who beat you up. She gave me my first key, my first clue that white people were human.

But I didn't keep that key very long, because I started working for the Army during the war. I was working for the first time with Southerners, and I had just never, never encountered this kind of madness before. I was a street boy; I grew up in Harlem. When you're small you've got to be quick and fairly agile and sharp-tongued, and you just didn't let anybody get away with anything, because you'd be dead if you did. So I walked around New Jersey working for the Army with people from Georgia, Alabama, Mississippi. I talked the way I always talked, acted the way I always acted, and I just couldn't believe what happened—the kind of fury that erupted. I told a white man from Georgia once that he was a liar. I wasn't being particularly hostile; I was just—

MEAD: You just thought he was a liar.

BALDWIN: I just thought that he was a liar and told him so. I'll never forget his face. It turned purple. It was the first time I was ever scared in my life, I must say, by another human being. But I saw something happen in his face: first it turned purple, then it turned absolutely white, and something happened in his eyes. I realized I was looking at death. That man wanted to kill me. If I had been alone I think he would have. And he was a much older man than I. I was only seventeen years old; he was about fifty. But a seventeen-year-old boy, because he was black, had managed to overturn his whole universe and he was about to kill me. That was my first rehearsal. That whole year, that whole time, is something that I've never been able to write about.

When I went south, I was a grown man. By this time— it's funny—I had a double reaction. I found myself in Montgomery, Alabama, and it wasn't the spirit of the people which was different or which surprised me, because by the time I was thirty-one I had given up expecting sanity from most white Americans. Essentially, I knew most white Americans were trapped in some stage of infantilism which wouldn't allow them to look at me as though I were a human being like themselves. I didn't expect them to. But I didn't expect what I found in the South, either. What happened to you is almost exactly what happened to me. I felt that I was walking on this rug, this wall-to-wall carpet. Beneath it is a complex system of wires, and one of those wires, if you step on it, will blow up the whole house.

MEAD: That's right.

BALDWIN: And everybody in the South knows where that wire is except me. I've got to cross this rug, too. But I don't know how I'm going to get across it, because every step I take is loaded with danger. Every time I open my mouth I'm wrong. The way I look at people is wrong. The way I sound is wrong. I am obviously not only a stranger in town, I'm an enemy. I've arrived with a bomb, because I'm a black from America *in* America.

MEAD: You're endangering everybody.

BALDWIN: I'm also endangering everybody else, which gives
you another fear. Then you really get scared. When I
worked with Medgar Evers for a little while, I would
never dare open my mouth in front of other people
around him. If he were working on a case or talking with
white or black people, I wouldn't open my mouth because
I had a Northern accent and I didn't know what that
would trigger in the minds and hearts of the people he
was talking to and what kind of danger it might place him
in. He was already, God knows, in enough danger.

That's a grim, grim pathology. The situation forces you,
the black cat in it, to become a party to it, whether you
like it or not. You cannot escape the pathology of a country in which you're born. You can resist it, you can react
to it, you can do all kinds of things, but you're trapped in
it. And your frame of reference is also the frame of reference of white people, no matter how you yourself try to
deal with it. No matter what you tell your children, you're
trapped: the despised darker brother in this great white
man's house.

And the great, great problem then is how you are going
to liberate yourself, first of all in the mind. Every objective fact which surrounds you simply bears witness to
your degradation. And how in the world are you going to
teach your child to grow up as a man when he sees daily
how little anyone respects your manhood? The kid knows
very well.

I knew it. I didn't know, I couldn't say, when my father
came home from work, what my father's working day was
like, but I did know that my father put on his bowler hat
and his white shirt and his dark preacher's uniform every
morning the Lord sent him, and with his little black lunch
box in his hand he went someplace downtown, went to

Long Island, where he was working in some factory, doing the most awful kind of hard labor. He made twenty-seven dollars and fifty cents a week all the years that I knew him. And he had nine children. He couldn't feed them, and of course he went—it was absolutely inevitable he would go mad.

How could he bear it? You can't quit the job if you've got those kids to feed. Your wife knows what you're going through, and if she loves you that makes it worse, because there is so little you can do to protect her. Your children are growing up and they begin to despise you, because they don't think you're a man. And you find yourself, because you happen to be born in the United States of America about two thousand years too early—

MEAD: I don't think it's that long.

BALDWIN: Well, two thousand or two hundred or twenty, it doesn't make any difference if it's one man's life. You go under. The crime or the pathology, which come to the same thing, is that it was not, it *is* not, being done by accident. It is not bizarre; it is *not* something like an act of God. It is something that has been done deliberately and is *being* done deliberately.

MEAD: Well, you know, I think you've got to stop there and think a little bit about history. Just consider for a minute if we never invented boats.

BALDWIN: Yes, where would England be.

MEAD: If we never invented boats, we would never have the problem we have today. If everybody had to walk, because they couldn't walk very far in a lifetime, they would stop and make love to the local girls. And gradually they would have moved from Africa, over Europe, getting paler and paler. But it would take a thousand years, and by the time they got to Sweden and got those pale blue eyes, and light skin so that they would enjoy what sun there was, because there wasn't much there—now, it would have taken thousands of years, and it would have been imperceptible. From the blackest group in Africa all the way up to the blond people up in Scandinavia.

But you see what happened was boats. And people are always taking boats and tearing along coasts and across seas, putting people side by side that contrast so sharply. Now, I think, we have talked a lot in this country. . . . One of the things I'm not sure of is whether it is one of the things worth discussing here—about generations— but in one way you and I belong to the same generation, in that we're prewar.

BALDWIN: We're pre-atomic age.

MEAD: These are the things we thought about and talked about. And they used to say children don't have any race prejudice. We heard that until the sacred cows screamed.

BALDWIN: "We've got to be taught to hate."

MEAD: That's what people said, that race feeling is all learned. Well, it isn't. It's true, you've got to be taught to *hate,* but the appreciation and fear of difference is every-where.

BALDWIN: That's right.

MEAD: And I've seen—plenty of people in this country have seen a white child who got used to a black face and black hands, and then the black person took off his shirt and they screamed because they sort of thought that this black face and black hands belonged to a white body. But I've seen a black child do the same thing with a white man— *scream* with fear—because, you know, there *is* a conspic-uous difference between a black skin and a white skin. In New Guinea the children scream with fear when they first see white people, just as much as white people scream with fear, because the contrast is too great. What we did on this earth with ships was to travel great distances. You could pick up people and take them far away, and as a result we've got these tremendous contrasts that try the souls of people. I think you've got to realize one other thing about white people, and that is that a white skin is a terrible temptation.

BALDWIN: How do you mean, exactly? But I think I know what you mean.

MEAD: Because we look like angels, you know that?

BALDWIN: I was going to get to that. Go on.

MEAD: You see, when those Angles from England were taken to Rome to be sold as slaves—were being sold as slaves in the marketplace—and a pope came along and looked at these slaves and he said, "What are they called?" and somebody said Angles and he said, "Oh, no, not Angles, angels. . . ." Now that meant way back when Christianity was a Mediterranean religion. But angels were white. The dead, you see, are white everywhere, because the bones are white and people associate the dead with skeletons and ghosts. Then you have angels and they are white. Now you get a group of people coming along—

BALDWIN: Who are also white.

MEAD: When the first people landed in Australia, the Australian aborigines thought they were the ghosts of their ancestors coming back. When Cortez landed in Mexico, he was greeted as the fair god; as far as we know there had never been any white people there. This was a dream of the dead. Now, it is not good for people's character—

BALDWIN: To be identified with angels.

MEAD: —to look like angels; it makes them behave very badly.

BALDWIN: That's very strange, because the root of it is some-where there, it seems to me, and that's deeper, I suppose, isn't it, than one would like to think?

MEAD: That's terribly, terribly deep, I think.

BALDWIN: Deeper than churches.

MEAD: But you know, there is something else about it, too. That is, it makes a difference whether you say white or light or bright. Funny, they all rhyme!

BALDWIN: Yes. "Light, bright and damn near white."

MEAD: You see, I've lived in a place where there wasn't any fire unless you make it with two little pieces of wood, a fire plow. People guard fire very carefully in such a place. And there is no light at night but the little embers of the fire, and you're terribly afraid. You can't make light easily; there is only a little spot of light in the darkness, and so people have been afraid of the dark always.

BALDWIN: Which is also identified with what? With death?

MEAD: Well, you see, with danger.

BALDWIN: With danger, yes.

MEAD: With danger. With terrible danger. Thieves come out of the night when there isn't any moon. Headhunters raid the camps. Wild beasts are only held off by the fire. When there is a moon it is lovely; you can dance all night. But when there is no moon the thieves get you. The en-emy gets you. Anything can get you. You don't know what.

Now I think electric lights are going to get rid of that one. Our children aren't afraid of the dark, not the ones who have lived in the city with electric lights. They press a button and the world is flooded, and they don't ever have to grow up with a fear of the dark.

BALDWIN: All that's very gloomy, in a way. It's going to be a

very long time before we conquer what is essentially a
tribal—

MEAD: It is before tribalism. This is, you know, just people's
feeling about the way they look themselves. Then you get
the contrast between black and white in the same group.

There was a little albino girl in Samoa, and they used to
call her my sister. She had pink eyes and pale, blemished
skin. To them she looked like me. And there is a strain of
people in Samoa with honey-colored hair. Fathers used to
grow their daughters' hair and sell it for wigs. Everybody
made wigs of this honey-colored hair because people
thought it was so beautiful. This went way back before
there were any white people there at all. And everywhere
one goes there are such contrasts. Now, when it's a little
contrast it doesn't matter, but when it is a big contrast
people do—

BALDWIN: But nobody knows where they come from really.
That's why we have so many—

MEAD: I noticed you used the word . . . something about
dark deeds.

BALDWIN: That's right. You know, I'm obviously—

MEAD: You're speaking "bloody English."

BALDWIN: I'm working in the English language, yes.

MEAD: But we find it also in African languages, you see.
That's the thing that's so strange.

BALDWIN: Yes, or else not strange. That's what you're saying.

MEAD: Well, what I'm saying is it's understandable that this
association of white and good and ghosts and all of these
things. . . . And now there are other people: Alvin—

BALDWIN: Poussaint, the black psychiatrist.

MEAD: He makes a great deal about the association between
black and dirt.

BALDWIN: Yes, I know another psychiatrist who does, too.

MEAD: But I don't think that's nearly as important. I think the point is brightness versus darkness and the fear of the dark. My little girl once said, "What's fear, what does it mean to be afraid?" She had never recognized anything to be afraid of, and I took her by the hand and stood her in the doorway of a totally dark room. "Look in there," I said. "That's what people mean when they say they're afraid." So I think that one has to consider that white people—Europeans, and this is all Europeans—I mean, just as you recognized in your book, that all Europeans have a deadly temptation to feel a sense of biological superiority.

BALDWIN: What you're saying comes close to suggesting that one of the reasons for the riddle of white supremacy is that all of a sudden there is some universal impulse to identify with light and fire. It is not merely historical—

MEAD: Universal perception.

BALDWIN: Yes. It is not merely an historical or theological aberration, let's say, but it comes out as something profound in everybody's nature.

MEAD: In everybody's nature.

BALDWIN: That's a weird and frightening perspective, isn't it, in a way?

MEAD: You see, I think it can be eliminated, now that we don't have to be afraid of the dark.

BALDWIN: Of course, but we have so many other things to be afraid of.

MEAD: Yes, but just the same, if brightness is something everybody can have from the time they're born—

BALDWIN: But it will be a long time before brightness becomes something everybody can have from the day they're born.

MEAD: We're all moving that way. Most people have electricity, acquaintance with electric lights. In the past no one knew that there was such a thing as immediate light flooding the world with brightness. A bunch of burning coconut leaves doesn't light anything. You know, it just makes a spot. There is no—

BALDWIN: It doesn't illuminate.

MEAD: No illumination.

BALDWIN: White people are in some sense a kind of tragic case.

MEAD: Yes, but you see it's a part of you also. Of course, in any oppressive situation both groups suffer, the oppressors and the oppressed. The oppressed suffer physically: they are frightened, they're abused, they're poor. But the oppressors suffer morally.

BALDWIN: Which is a worse kind of suffering.

MEAD: Because they have to deny something in themselves. Now, one of the things I wanted to ask you about. . . . I took a friend of mine who lives in Paris to the performance of Genet's *The Blacks* that was given over here. He had seen the performance that was given at the Musée de l'Homme, which was acted by Africans, young Africans—anthropologists, I suppose—and he said it was a sacrament of hate.

BALDWIN: Really?

MEAD: You know, when they gave it over here they kept clowning all the time. Did you see it?

BALDWIN: I saw it here, yes. St. Marks Playhouse.

MEAD: It was just on the edge of clowning all the time.

BALDWIN: Yes, that's true.

MEAD: And they were just the poorest haters I've ever seen loose. They really were!

BALDWIN: That's true. I think that Jean Genet's *Blacks* on some level is a very frightening play. It is a very intimidat-

ing play. I was somewhat involved with the production in
New York because I knew the director and I knew a lot of
people in the cast, and I was over there a few times during rehearsal. I realized that many of the black people in
the cast were—or all the black people in the cast had
. . . how can I put this?—were not exactly ashamed, but
there was something in Genet's tone—

MEAD: That was wrong for them.

BALDWIN: There was something that was merciless in the
tone of the play and the perceptions of the play. It's a
very black play indeed, a much blacker play than any
American I know of would be able to conceive or write.

MEAD: That's right.

BALDWIN: *Nobody* gets away, the way he structured it. It's
just an absolutely grim circle which is going to go on and
on and on and on forever, according to Genet. Whether
one agrees with this or not is not the point.

MEAD: But that's what the play is.

BALDWIN: And in order to play it you have to reach a level in
yourself which not many people are able to do, really.
And the reason I think that it was always on the edge of
clowning is because the people in the play, even unconsciously, and perhaps the director too, even unconsciously, had to protect themselves against this really
ghastly vision in which everybody after all is utterly con-
demned. You know, there isn't anybody in that play worth
anything. They're all absolute monsters and horrors. And
you have a terrible suspicion that maybe Genet is right;
certainly there's very little in the course of human history
to indicate that he's wrong. But that strips the whole
question of color, perhaps very healthfully, I think.

MEAD: I am not absolutely sure about hating at that level.

Do you think the same actors today would be able to face that much hate? I'm inclined—

BALDWIN: I don't think so. But I'm not sure the problem in the play is hate. I think it may be history.

MEAD: —to think that there might be different actors doing it. Something happened. This again is more about the South than it is about the North. What one does in this country in trying to understand the contrast between the two, of course . . . I think it is much easier to regard the South as another nation. It's just completely another culture, but both are part of our national consciousness. Every Northerner has the South in him, too. And, of course, every Southerner has the North in him, the feel of the conqueror's heel and what it did to the South and all that.

Now, up to about thirty years ago there really were no black people in the South who hadn't received some kindness from white people. There were hardly any black doctors then, or black teachers, or black dentists, or black trained nurses; Huey Long got black nurses into the hospitals by making speeches about all the white nurses nursing black people. Almost everywhere—unless you lived in the very far reaches of some rural area—black people had their wounds bound up by white people.

BALDWIN: And vice versa.

MEAD: It isn't quite vice versa, because there were these pockets of poor whites where there were no blacks at all. These poor whites were caught in the middle because the blacks despised them and the other whites despised them. They just didn't have any life at all. In 1942 I started saying, "We've got to hurry, while there are still people who—"

BALDWIN: Remember this. The kindness.

MEAD: —who remember this, and who have received kindness from each other's hands.

BALDWIN: That's not true anymore. It's not true at all.

MEAD: That's it, you see. This is the thing that's happened. In institutions like Hampton Institute, with its middle-class black students—some quite wealthy—there are many, I believe, who never received a kindness from a white person in their whole lives.

BALDWIN: Didn't know any white people personally—in fact, at all.

MEAD: Never saw them, and this scared them. When they come out into the white world they're able to hate them because they are hating a stranger, and it's very easy to hate a stranger. But it's hard to hate the thing that's close to you, and this was the South thirty years ago.

BALDWIN: Until thirty years ago.

MEAD: Until we began getting a whole educated group of black doctors, black lawyers—

BALDWIN: Until the Second World War, which altered the economy. It shifted everybody's relations and made the whole patriarchal thing, which is what we are essentially talking about, obsolete. It became obsolete nearly overnight.

MEAD: And the style that those actors were still acting in when they gave *The Blacks* was in the old style of black-white relations.

BALDWIN: I don't know what would happen if one did that play now. There's a very unfortunate sentimentality that surrounds the whole question of color in America. It's unfortunate. And *The Blacks* is not in the least sentimental. Yet everyone in America, including black people, has always on some level—or, if not always, often—been necessarily blinded by a kind of hope which was simply sentimental, in that it did not refer to reality. Even the civil rights movement was stained with a kind of sentimentality which sometimes drove me nearly mad. I admired those kids very much. I thought that everybody was possessed with tremendous devotion and tremendous belief. Yet it is a very sentimental country. The American consciousness is sentimental in just as bad a way as the German consciousness, which means that they never see anything clearly. This applies to black people, too. Now I think something else is happening. I think now with *The Blacks* it might . . . the production might err in the direction of a kind of sentimentality of rage.

MEAD: It would still be sentimental.

BALDWIN: It would still be sentimental.

MEAD: You know, I put your kind of writing beside Louise Bogan or Will Gibson. They both happen to be Irish people who as children had a living language around them and then just went in and got English literature from nowhere. Louise Bogan's parents were hardly literate, and she used to say that when she was sixteen she walked into the Boston Public Library and took Keats off the shelf.

BALDWIN: It's almost exactly what I did.

MEAD: First you had the liveliness of a living language around you. I think that's necessary. But then you hadn't been corrupted by anything low-level or any nonsense in between, really.

BALDWIN: That's very true. I never thought about it quite that way until much, much later. But in the very beginning I was surrounded by the people in the church and all that music and all that fantastic imagery. Of course, as a kid you don't react to it that way, but it's in you.

MEAD: All the way inside.

BALDWIN: I used to tell my mother, when I was little, "When I grow up I'm going to do this or do that. I'm going to be a great writer and buy you this and buy you that." And she would say, very calmly, very dryly, "It's more than a notion." That kind of dry understatement which characterizes so much of black speech in America is my key to something, only I didn't know it then.

Then I started reading. I read everything I could get my hand on, murder mysteries, *The Good Earth*, everything. By the time I was thirteen I had read myself out of Harlem. There were two libraries in Harlem, and by the time I was thirteen I had read every book in both libraries and I had a card downtown for Forty-second Street, which is where I first encountered a white policeman. But that's another story.

But that has a lot to do with—what I had to do then was bring the two things together: the possibilities the books suggested and the impossibilities of the life *around* me. Of course, by this time I was in some kind of collision without quite knowing it, with the assumptions of the . . . what we will call the master language and the facts of life as it, life, was being presented to me. Dickens meant a lot to me, for example, because there was a rage in Dickens which was also in me.

MEAD: Well, the subject matter—

BALDWIN: And *Uncle Tom's Cabin* meant a lot to me because there was a rage in her which was somehow in me. Something I recognized without knowing what I recognized, if you know what I mean.

Later on, when I went away to Paris and found myself, I had to think all this through. I found myself in Paris partly because I realized that I couldn't live in America on the assumptions by which I lived really, and quite uncon-

sciously because. . . . I was very young, and the assumptions of the people by whom I was surrounded, who now
were white people, were so fatally different that I was
really in trouble. I was in danger of *thinking* myself out of
existence, because a black, an unknown helpless black
boy, wandering around the way I did and thinking the
way I thought, was obviously a dangerous kind of freak.
Obviously, you say what you think, and there is no way to
hide what you think. People look at you with great wonder and great hostility, and I got scared because I could
see that I wouldn't be able to function in this world or
even in this language, and I went away.

But I began to think in French. I began to understand
the English language better than I ever had before; I
began to understand the English language which I came
out of, the language that produced Ray Charles or Bessie
Smith or which produced all the poets who produced me.
A kind of reconciliation began which could not have happened if I had not stepped out of the English language.
It's a very strange kind of odyssey, but I think in one way
it explains a lot about Black American literature.

For the sake of argument there are two kinds of
poets: the kind of respectable poet represented by Coun-
tee Cullen, who essentially used a borrowed idiom and
did very interesting things with it, but very minor things,
and a poet like Gwendolyn Brooks, who really picks up
her language out of the streets. She knows Shakespeare
and Blake and Milton and she can make marvelous allit-
erations and marvelous ironies and perceptions, because
she lives in both languages. In a sense she's creating—and
that's what you're doing anyway if you're a writer—in a
sense re-creating the language.

But you can only re-create it out of human speech, so

in a sense black poets are putting, for the first time in the history of the world, the experience of black people into what has been essentially a white language. It's one of the great unconscious contributions America has made, because the way Americans speak is really tremendously influenced and stained by their relationship to black men. It has made a whole new language which doesn't yet exist, for example, in England or anywhere else where English is spoken. And black people elsewhere in the world—I began to realize when I was in London and Africa—black people who come from the colonies are just beginning to feel not exactly at home in the West but uneasy in the West.

MEAD: They learned either French or English as an academic foreign language, and it didn't have the same meaning for them.

BALDWIN: It didn't have the same meaning at all. And also they were in another situation: They were born in a situation in which everyone they saw was black, except maybe the Governor General. So it was much harder for a black man born as a British subject to apprehend where he really was and where the power really was. It wasn't until he came to London, for the most part, that he discovered that he was not free—this freedom which had been the myth on the island or in the colony, because the English, and the French, too, had the good sense to have all kinds of figureheads.

But when he found himself in London he discovered—and it's a very difficult moment to go through—that he was not English, that London was his only metropole and no one wanted him in London. He had no future in the English language, but he had no future in the past either, because once you leave you cannot really go back. You can go back only on certain limited terms.

There is a sense in which I could say I never have left Harlem. But there is another sense in which I certainly never can go back there, if only because the Harlem in which I was born exists no longer. And though that rupture has something to do with race, it also has something to do with a nature or quality or the specialness—I don't know what the word is—of human experience. Because in my case, as in the case of the boy who comes to London, you have the choice of accepting without question the gift of the language, the gift of the culture, the dominant culture, in which case you must betray your mother, your father, your brothers, or you can turn away from it, going back to your mother, father and brothers and becoming absolutely useless. Because you cannot go back, as I said. And the only other thing you can do is try to take from your own culture what you need, drag with you what you need from where you've come.

Then you have to pay great attention both to the people above you and the people beside you, who are, in effect, beneath you—beneath you because they would appear to be less well armed, culturally. You're in a kind of limbo until you begin to work that out, and it's a longer process than I would have thought because a lot of the kids I see in London now remind me of what I was like, let us say, when I was fourteen. You know, what Malcolm X was like when he was conking his hair and lindy-hopping around Detroit and learning all, as he thought, the white man's tricks. But, of course, when you're learning tricks you look like you're learning tricks. The clothes don't fit, the hair is not right, it is not yet yours. And the

American black is probably the only person who's made
that particular journey.

MEAD: English is his mother tongue.

BALDWIN: And he was born in the West.

MEAD: Yes, born in the West and this is his mother tongue.

BALDWIN: But New York is not my metropole. It's the city in
which I was born. It's my city. The city belongs to me as
much as it belongs to anybody else in this country. London also belongs to the black people, who paid as much
for it, God knows, as any white Englishman did.

MEAD: But they weren't born there.

BALDWIN: They weren't born there. It's an entirely different
relationship, and it will take a long, long time to work
itself out. Essentially the same thing is happening in
France. It's happening all over the Western world. It
wouldn't be so sinister in so many ways if the Western
world were brighter or if the Eastern world were more
attractive.

MEAD: But you know, I want to go back to talk about the
Republic of South Africa, because the South Africans are
the only white people who belong on the African continent. And they belong there. They were driven out of
France after the massacre of St. Bartholomew; they were
made homeless. They went to Holland and learned Dutch
but were abominably treated by the Dutch, so Dutch isn't
their mother tongue either. They've been displaced and
displaced.

They went to Africa, and it was an almost empty country. There was hardly anybody there at all, neither black
nor white, just a very few nomadic people. Most of the
blacks moved down later. Then the whites fought for this
country, and they *thought* they had a country. This is
what I hear in the voice—and it's not in people who speak

Afrikaans; it's in English-speaking South Africans—when I hear the words "my country." You hear it also in the voices of people from new countries who are worried about the state of their country.

BALDWIN: Worried about the way the country is treated and what people think about it.

MEAD: And they're on a continent that everybody thinks belongs to blacks, the way everybody thinks Europe belongs to whites.

BALDWIN: I understand them very well, I think. But of course it's unacceptable. The regime is unacceptable.

MEAD: Oh, the regime is frightful.

BALDWIN: They may turn out to be the most spectacular victims of the doctrine of white supremacy that the world has ever seen, because obviously they cannot liberate themselves from it.

MEAD: They have nowhere to go; they burned all their boats. When they got out of the Commonwealth they acted like these people who believe the Second Coming of Christ is coming now. You give all your clothes away and all your money away and get up on the roof wrapped in sheets, and it has got to come. It's got to come, because there is nowhere to go.

BALDWIN: But it doesn't come. It's not going to come.

MEAD: Then it's necessary to think comparatively of all of these positions around the world; it's necessary to think about all the different groups in the Caribbean—how different they are and what they bring into the country— then to look at the former British Guiana—where black people had higher status than Indians—Indians from India.

BALDWIN: Yes, you have similar situations in some of the

African nations, at least on the west coast where the Lebanese—

MEAD: Are being treated badly.

BALDWIN: Or being driven out.

MEAD: Being driven out and treated frightfully.

BALDWIN: And it's very hard. One's got to disengage one's self from any kind of sentimentality. One's got to try to understand what is really happening in this century. The greatest sentimentality which both black and white have shared for years is the notion that black people are somehow different from white people. We are different in some ways but, alas, there is one level on which people are not different and that's the level on which they are wicked. There again you can say that all men are brothers. We've got to be as clear-headed about human beings as possible, because we are still each other's only hope.

MEAD: I think there is even a difference in wickedness in different cultures. For instance, when the English get angry they get colder and colder and colder. Now when Americans get angry, black or white, they don't get colder—

BALDWIN: No, they get hotter.

MEAD: They get hotter and they yell and there's a real difference.

When the Irish get angry they're in love. It was one of the things that I used to watch with my child when we shared a household with a family where the wife was Irish. She treated my daughter beautifully, but she didn't love her quite as much as she loved her own son. So my daughter was beginning to learn that anger and love are the same thing, which she wasn't supposed to learn, because she wasn't Irish, after all. As in Kipling's poem, "For where there are Irish, there's loving and fighting,

And when we stop either, it's Ireland no more! Ireland no more!" So there is really a difference, even in anger, and anger then can lead to cruelty between one group and another.

Now one thing I'd like to ask you about is the whole role of touch. It seems to me that the average middle-class American is exceedingly inhibited about touching other people.

BALDWIN: He's frozen, really.

MEAD: He's frozen. He maybe shakes hands.

BALDWIN: Even that is done nervously.

MEAD: He doesn't really enjoy it. Now my general experience in working with black people is that I always have to touch them, or they touch me, if we are going to get anywhere.

BALDWIN: Oh, yeah.

MEAD: I feel, if I don't touch them, I haven't communicated with them at all. I could sit across the room and make beautiful speeches forever, but one touch makes the difference, just one touch.

BALDWIN: I don't know why that is. I remember once in Africa I watched the way Africans carried their babies; they wrapped them in this thing on their backs. Somebody said it's almost the key to the African psychology, because when the baby needs something all the baby's got to do is knock.

MEAD: And you can't *see* it, you see.

BALDWIN: You can only feel it and react to its movements. That's a very subtle thing, isn't it? And it's not typical of life in the West; it's typical of the life I lived. We all grew up on top of each other, slapping each other or kissing each other or whatever. But we always touched each other, so we all touched everybody else.

However, it's one of the terrible inhibitions of middle-class black people. You go to some middle-class black person's rather elegant, upper-class, middle-class party—they are ghastly parties—and everybody is being more rigid than any Englishman or white American would be, because, as I said before, they're learning tricks. Then about two o'clock in the morning, if you can stay that long, somebody will break down and presently everybody will end up in the kitchen. You see, after all the stiffest black people have gone home, the hostess or the host will go into the kitchen and take out some chicken and we'll take off our shoes and revert to our savage ways and have a ball, just being with each other and being ourselves.

MEAD: Well, one of the important things, it seems to me, one of the very important things in this country, is when black people touch white people freely. This is what has happened. You may feel that everything has gotten worse. But I walk around the world as a white person. So does my sister, and she says the same thing. She's taught in Harlem, taught all over New York City. Today sometimes when she's lame and carries a cane—today a black man will take her arm and help her across the street.

BALDWIN: That's always been true in America.

MEAD: Not quite. The initiative to touch was always reserved. There was always a line that might be dangerous. But I think it's just as important that black people feel perfectly free to touch white people, because if they don't touch people they're not human.

BALDWIN: Not touching a person is a way of rejecting him. And it's also a way of being rejected. I remember when I was much younger, when I was in junior high school and also in the pulpit, I went through great traumas. I was about fourteen and was taught by my mother to always stand up on subways and give a seat to a woman. But some of the preachers told me that I should never give my seat to a white woman. This gave me a tremendous conflict for a while, because standing up for a white woman would have seemed to be an act of servility. I solved this problem very neatly by never sitting down in the subway. But it was traumatic because I had to think about it and think it through for myself and decide whether a woman's color is more important than the fact that she's a woman. You get over it, but I think that every black person must have gone through this kind of private warfare, especially a black man.

Being black. Black. Black. That's another aspect of this whole thing that no one has ever really dealt with! What it means has been suggested by many people, but it has never really been apprehended. It's a very complex situation when a black boy grows into a man and finds himself in this country. His sexuality is menaced from the moment his eyes open on the world. And the only person who really knows anything about that, who knows it most intimately, is also the most dangerous figure in his life—his mother. His father, for the most part, has no relationship to his kid anyway. Also, it's not something his father can do much about, because his own manhood is menaced and he's facing knives every day, partly to feed the child. So it evolves upon the mother to invest the child, her man child, with some kind of interior dignity which will protect him against something he really can't be protected against, unless he has some interior thing within him to meet it.

In my own experience I did a lot of dodging and side-stepping, but I had to do a great deal of frontal attacking, too. Part of the great dilemma was how in the world, first of all, to treat a black woman. When I was growing up one was very ambivalent about being black at all, and one knew nothing about oneself, and this was not one's fault. The schools I'd been to, the books I'd read, the people I knew didn't know anything about themselves either, and to find out about myself I had to do several difficult things. But how to deal with a black girl whom you knew you couldn't protect unless you were prepared to work all your life in the post office, unless you were prepared to make bargains I was temperamentally unfitted to make?

And even then it wouldn't have worked. It didn't work. I could see that all around me. I could see the price some black people paid, some great black men had paid. They were quite extraordinary and very difficult, difficult men, though they weren't difficult with me, because they loved me. But they were very, very up tight. *Nobody* in his right mind was going to say the wrong word to them on *any* Tuesday unless he wanted to die.

Then there's the great problem of white women. They come to you for the most part as though you're some exotic—well, they really come to you as though you're some *extraordinary* phallic symbol.

MEAD: As if you're nothing but a phallic symbol.

BALDWIN: As if you're nothing but a walking phallus.

MEAD: You don't have a head.

BALDWIN: No, no head, no arms, no nothing, just a . . . and of course you can do that for a while. But you end up —well, actually the act of love becomes an act of murder in which you are also committing suicide. In my case, I simply split the scene completely. I went to another country about five minutes before I would have been carried off to Bellevue.

I got to France, and everything came pouring out. I

started breaking up bars, knocking down people. I spent a year in Paris tearing up the town. Of course, I got torn up too, finally ended up in jail. It took a year—to get to jail, I mean. Even when I was doing it I realized what was happening, but I couldn't stop it. I knew it all finally had to come out. And finally, when I was *absolutely* flat on my back and kind of humiliated with myself because I knew I had behaved very badly, it was over. Something was over.

The trap is, if you're born into that situation, the nature of the trap is with your not even knowing it, acquiescing. You've been taught that you're inferior and so you act as though you're inferior. And on the level that is very difficult to get at, you really believe it. And, of course, all the things you do to prove you're not inferior only really prove you are. They boomerang.

MEAD: Yes, if you're paying attention.

BALDWIN: You're playing the game according to somebody else's rules, and you can't win until you understand the rules and step out of that particular game, which is not, after all, worth playing.

MEAD: You know, I thought it would be worthwhile to think a little bit about the parallelism between race and sex and where this exists and where it doesn't. Ralph Bunche and I used to laugh because there were parts of the Cosmos Club he couldn't go in and there were parts I couldn't go in. They were different, but both our exclusion was based on prejudice.

Now the thing that Women's Lib is talking about at the moment, of course, is that women have accepted a male version of themselves. And when you're talking about writing, what language are you going to write in? Robert Browning wrote, "Teach me, only teach, Love! As I ought I will speak thy speech, Love, Think thy thought." The

whole of Elizabeth Barrett Browning's life was just acting
out his image of her.

And then you get Olive Schreiner or Emily Dickinson
struggling with images that are really not feminine and
not doing it very well, because they had to take their
whole lives virtually—

BALDWIN: Apart.

MEAD: And work on developing new images because they
weren't there for them in literature.

BALDWIN: That's what black people have to do, too.

MEAD: And there is the kind of relationship of accepting, of
using a language that wasn't written, wasn't made for you.

BALDWIN: Wasn't written with you in mind, and you've simply got to force the language to pay attention to you in
order to exist in it, and you have no choice but to exist in
it. Even if you manage to learn Swahili, still you need the
English language to do all the things which have yet to be
done in this terrifying century. The whole race-sex thing
is probably in that area where one can locate the microbe.
But it is almost impossible to do, because both areas are
so inaccessible to the memory and so wounding to the ego
that you have to go through extraordinary excavations
with your own shovel and your own guts to be able to
come anywhere near the truth about the connection between your rage, for example, and your sexuality. You
know, the proximity in your sexuality.

MEAD: I think this is what's happening with Women's Lib.
Maybe one could say that there's a kind of parallel, that in
a sense the young black man in this country who's an-
guished is the one who in a way has had the most oppor-
tunity.

BALDWIN: Well, that's another way of saying that one feels
most cheated.

MEAD: To be given a little bit of hope, to be given access, yes; so then he feels most cheated. Well, you see, women have been educated just like boys theoretically.

BALDWIN: But I don't think that's really possible.

MEAD: They've tried it. They wore blue jeans and they went to school with boys and they were given the same education. It's as if you said to a man, "What are you going to be?" and he said, "Well, I think I'll be a lawyer unless I get married." "What do you mean, unless you get married?" "Well, if I get married I'll have to have a chicken farm." "Why do you have to have a chicken farm?" "It's so good for children to be brought up on a chicken farm." This is the kind of thing that we ask of women, to give up a part of themselves when they marry.

I wonder also if it's worth saying, since you're talking about what the mother gave the black boy, I wonder if it's worth saying that the women who are angry are the daughters of fathers who have destroyed their femininity, who have destroyed them as people by laughing at them as women.

BALDWIN: By patronizing them.

MEAD: Patronizing them and laughing at them and saying it's a pity that they're their little girls and—

BALDWIN: Of course, I think it's a symptom of a much deeper kind of distress. One of the things happening in this century is the tremendous upheaval caused by the history of the concept of color, but also something is happening now between the sexes. It has been happening for a long time, but now it is happening more overtly. It's difficult to articulate, but the relationship between the sexes, which has apparently never really been as fixed as everyone always claimed, is now very definitely in a state of flux, and women are reacting. Men and women are both reacting to it. In fact, it is very difficult for a man to know exactly what the terms are; to know how he is to be related to a woman. And it's very difficult for her to know on what terms she's to be related to him. And the institution of marriage, though people don't like to think so, is abruptly becoming obsolete. After all, it is no longer necessary for the perpetuation of—

MEAD: It's still necessary to bring up the children.

BALDWIN: Well, many people don't agree with that.

MEAD: Well, whatever they call it.

BALDWIN: I tend to agree with that. I think there has to be some kind of unit for the perpetuation—in fact, to protect the child—but I don't think it will be precisely what it has been heretofore. What it will be, I don't know.

MEAD: What has it been heretofore! It's been every kind of thing you can imagine.

BALDWIN: Yes, hasn't it.

MEAD: So that I think we'll still have the family to bring up children in.

BALDWIN: What about the socialist states?

MEAD: Socialist states all have the family. My goodness, the Russian family is one of the most conventional families in the world.

BALDWIN: It is? That's very reassuring, I suppose.

MEAD: Divorce is terribly hard to get in Russia; they found they couldn't get the kind of character they wanted without the family.

BALDWIN: Yes, without the mother.

MEAD: Without the mother and the father.

BALDWIN: Without the mother and the father, yes.

MEAD: So they went back to the old way, and now they blame the mother and father for everything that goes wrong.

BALDWIN: With the child?

MEAD: Yes. In Russia the parents get blamed for everything that goes wrong, and the Party gets complimented for everything that goes right.

BALDWIN: Ha, that's wild, that's funny.

MEAD: But people are making these points, I mean equating the black revolution and the women's revolution and the youth revolution. And I think it's probably important to see where they're related and where they're not. Now, as far as youth is concerned, everybody's going to get over being young. It's very trying while you're in it, but everybody is going to get older if they live.

BALDWIN: The youth revolution is . . . I hate to sound patronizing. I lived through youth; I was young, too, and it wasn't very different from the superficial symptoms of being young now. I mean, is there a great difference between being born in 1924 and being born after 1945?

MEAD: Oh, there's a generation gap in the world now.

BALDWIN: Yes, but—

MEAD: That caught the youth, but they're getting older now.

BALDWIN: Yes, but they're getting older according to terms which didn't exist when we were young.

MEAD: That's right.

BALDWIN: And we don't really know what those terms are.

MEAD: But that isn't really about youth, that's about people. Ten years from now they will be thirty-five and—

BALDWIN: Yes, but they'll still be living under the shadow of extinction. We weren't born under that shadow. Our minds weren't formed in the shadow of what is in effect an enormous betrayal. If I were young, if I had been born after Hiroshima, by the time I was fifteen I would have judged my elders very mercilessly indeed. I mean, the

world in which the post-Hiroshima generation was born
—and whether or not this difficult, protesting generation
is absolutely right is not terribly important—is a world for
which their parents are responsible. And what their parents have done is betrayed them and betrayed their future.

MEAD: Well, wait a minute! Let's just work on this point of
responsibility. It fits into all this, all these guilt statements. There are different ways of looking at guilt. In the
Eastern Orthodox faith, everybody shares the guilt of
creatureliness and the guilt for anything they ever
thought. Now, the Western Northern-European position
and the North American position on the whole is that
you're guilty for things that you did yourself and not for
things that other people did.

BALDWIN: Yes, but it seems to me that that's harder to establish.

MEAD: Why?

BALDWIN: For example, for a banal example, banal and perhaps romantic, take American society today. It's very difficult to find anybody who—and I think it's the nature of
modern society—voted for Nixon.

MEAD: Who what?

BALDWIN: Apparently no one in America voted for Nixon. At
least no one I've met.

MEAD: But an awful lot of people did.

BALDWIN: Well, somebody did.

MEAD: He got elected.

BALDWIN: But the terms of society are such that nobody
takes any responsibility. Perhaps nobody can take the responsibility for what is going on. If that's so, it's very
sinister. It reminds me a little bit of Germany in the years
of the Third Reich. Years and years later, when I went to

Germany and talked to any German—and I'm talking about people much older than myself who lived through the entire holocaust—one got the very distinct impression —and I said this and got into terrible fights in Germany— "You mean to tell me that six million Jews were murdered while the entire nation was out to lunch?"

Something like that is happening here. The trial of the Chicago Seven is an example. In my book it's another indefensible and obscene scandal. It's just so blatant. And, in my book, all the lies we've been told about all our assassinations are just too preposterous. I react by feeling that I'm being treated with tremendous contempt. If you tell me that James Earl Ray managed to blow Martin Luther King's head off in Memphis and then swam the river all the way to London by himself, I'm sorry. It's simply not to be considered for a moment. But this is happening in this society, and no one is taking any responsibility for it; and it seems to me that when that happens in a society, that society is on the edge of absolute chaos.

MEAD: I think you have to start first with the question of what would you have done if you had power at the time of the bomb? Most American people could not take any responsibility for it because they didn't know it existed.

BALDWIN: But they could have taken responsibility for the fact that the Japanese were interned and the Germans were not. They could have taken responsibility for that fact. And I saw it. I swear to you that when I was eighteen years old during that war—

MEAD: They weren't interned in Hawaii, where they were far more dangerous.

BALDWIN: They were interned in California.

MEAD: But not in Hawaii.

BALDWIN: Well, my point—

MEAD: There were Japanese people in New York State, where they never interned them. Now, are the people of New York State to take the guilt for the Californians or the credit for the good behavior of the Hawaiians? Which one are they responsible for?

BALDWIN: I don't know, but it happened in the same country.

MEAD: Yes, I know. But you see you've got two kinds of things here. You have the guilt of people who feel that they share the guilt of dropping the bomb. Now I am absolutely certain that if I had been asked I would have said not to drop it. I have no doubt and therefore I have no guilt.

BALDWIN: All right, I accept that, I accept that.

MEAD: None at all, you see. This is a Northern or Western view of guilt. I don't say because I'm an American I share the guilt of what the American government did when I didn't know it was doing it.

BALDWIN: That is true, that is true.

MEAD: All right, now when these children—these fifteen-year-olds you just made up—say their parents produced the bomb, they're mistaken. Their parents didn't produce the bomb. The bomb was produced by a very small number of people. It was produced within a context made up of complementary images. We had an image of what the Germans would have done—which in any kind of rational world they would have done but they didn't. So we produced the bomb we thought they were going to produce. This is a kind of frightful behavior.

Now, once we know about it, once the American people know about the bomb, then if they don't do anything about it I would say they're guilty. But I started interviewing about two hours after Hiroshima and I went to work immediately and I've been working ever since to make people understand what atomic war would mean. I don't feel guilty.

BALDWIN: I'm not talking about that kind of cosmic guilt for the human race. Actually I meant that if I were a child of this country I would judge my elders very harshly. Whether I would be wrong or right is scarcely at this time relevant. Because this is the world my elders have created. This is the world that they've created and this is the future—

MEAD: But one generation of them didn't create it. It was created by hundreds of generations.

BALDWIN: Of course. But a boy of fifteen doesn't have that perspective, does he? Martin Luther King discovered this himself when he finally went to Chicago: that there was a whole generation of black people whom he was completely unable to touch. Their lives, the lives of black boys in Chicago, were so much different from the lives of black boys in Montgomery, so much more fragmented and in so many ways so much more bitter.

It was so much more devious to say to one of those kids, "We shall overcome." To say that, with patience, time will do this or that was absolutely meaningless. The boy was standing on a street corner looking at his friends dying on the needle, possibly dying on the needle himself. He certainly had a friend in jail, certainly had a girl friend on the block, certainly knew the reasons for the lives led by his mother and his father. You couldn't go to a fifteen-, sixteen- or seventeen-year-old boy and say anything to him at all, except try to teach him something that he himself really wanted to learn. What you had to do was deal with him as though he were a valuable human being because no one had ever treated him as though he had any value.

Finally they began to do it themselves. That's how we got the Blackstone Rangers and that's how we finally got the Black Panthers. They could no longer turn to my generation for anything at all. They had to turn to themselves and therefore, in some sense, immobilize the members of my generation who were against them and enlist the aid of those members of my generation who understood or tried to understand what it meant to be in their shoes.

I have to understand that, despite the fact that I'm twenty-five years older, I'm still in their shoes. Because the police in this country do not make any distinction between a Black Panther or a black lawyer or my brother or me. The cops aren't going to ask me my name before they pull the trigger. I'm part of this society and I'm in exactly the same situation as anybody else—any other black person—in it. If I don't know that, then I'm fairly self-deluded. What I'm trying to get at is that whether the question of guilt—I'm not interested very much in the question of guilt. What I'm trying to get at is the question of responsibility. I didn't drop the bomb, either. And I never lynched anybody. Yet I am responsible not for what has happened but for what can happen.

MEAD: Yes, that's different. I think the responsibility for what can happen, which in a sense is good guilt—which is sort of a nonsensical term—

BALDWIN: Yes, but I know what you mean. It's useful guilt.

MEAD: Responsibility. It is saying I am going to make an effort to have things changed. But to take the responsibility for something that was done by others—

BALDWIN: Well, you can't do that.

MEAD: —by others, not myself.

BALDWIN: But again, just to belabor this, it took me a long time to realize that my father was not responsible for my condition. In the beginning I obviously thought you judge the person next to you, the nearest person. And many black people still blame their ancestors for getting on those boats at all. Of course that's preposterous, but it's part of the journey one makes.

MEAD: I think it's equally preposterous for you to blame your black ancestors for going on those boats or having sold somebody to get on those boats as it is to blame the white men who were slavers there for what is happening now. It's just preposterous to blame one's ancestors, because they were living in a situation—

BALDWIN: They were living within a certain framework and a certain set of principles.

MEAD: Now, back in 1944 I was head of what we called a school of community affairs, and we were dealing with cross-racial and cross-ethnic relationships, I was walking across the Wellesley campus with my four-year-old, who was climbing pine trees instead of keeping up with me.

I said, "You come down out of that pine tree. You don't have to eat pine needles like an Indian." So she came down and she asked, "Why do the Indians have to eat pine needles?" I said, "To get their Vitamin C, because they don't have any oranges." She asked, "Why don't they have any oranges?" Then I made a perfectly clear technical error; I said, "Because the white man took their land away from them." She looked at me and she said, "Am I white?" I said, "Yes, you are white." *"But I didn't took their land away from them, and I don't like it to be tooken!"* she shouted.

Now if I had said, "The early settlers took their land away," she wouldn't have said, "Am I an early settler?"

But I had made a blanket racial category: the white man.
It was a noble sentiment, but it was still racial sentiment.

BALDWIN: I'm very mistrustful of noble sentiments. But that
demands a level of clarity which has always been rare.

MEAD: The kids all say—and they're pretty clear about it—
that the future is now. It's no use predicting about the
year 2000.

BALDWIN: No.

MEAD: It's what we do this week that matters.

BALDWIN: Exactly.

MEAD: Right now, this minute.

BALDWIN: That's the only time there is; there isn't any other
time.

MEAD: Yes, that's right. So I'm very much in sympathy, and
I've been able to make the move to understand that black
power isn't a betrayal of the ideals of those of us who
worked for integration. A lot of people in my generation
fought hard for integration, especially down South. They
risked their lives for integration, and then everybody
turns around and says it was all wrong. It's hard on them.
I've been able to make the move to understanding black
power very easily, really, because I think it's a way in
which black people take charge of their own lives.

BALDWIN: That's all it means, really.

MEAD: That's all it means. To take charge of their own lives,
to give themselves the dignity of choice and movement,
and respect for themselves as what they are.

BALDWIN: Then they can decide who they want to be friends
with.

MEAD: Yes, from a position of strength, in a sense. I mean,
they are still a minority and they are still pushed around,
but nevertheless they've got a position of strength. But if
we are going to have to continually go back and go back

and go back over the past, I don't know how we're going
to escape from it.

BALDWIN: Well, we won't be able to use the past. I know
exactly what you mean. But you are talking, we both are,
of a perspective which most people never achieve. For
example, I know that the President of this nation doesn't
have any such perspective. Ronald Reagan doesn't have
any such perspective. Most of the people in the streets
don't. The taxi driver doesn't. Of course, it's just a useless
complaint, because if that's the way it is, that's simply the
way it is. It requires people like you and people like myself to insist on some kind of coherence. If one has
enough respect for human beings—and ultimately I do—
one believes that they would prefer not to be wicked.

MEAD: I think there are awfully few people who enjoy being
wicked.

BALDWIN: I think that's rare, too, thank God. But I do think,
especially in this century of displaced people and wander-
ers, that everyone is an exile. The whole concept of nations is becoming, no matter whether one likes it or not,
obsolete before our eyes. It doesn't make any difference
anymore whether you were born in Germany or Switzerland or France. Everyone has been hounded all over the
world, from pillar to post. Everyone's become an exile.

MEAD: Everyone's an exile. They haven't found a home on
earth yet.

BALDWIN: Yes, that's what I'm really trying to get at, and
that means some radical alteration in all of our social arrangements, social and economic arrangements. And no
one seems equipped at the moment to even envision
them, much less to—

MEAD: But everybody's got to grow up initially at home,

accepting the physique of his own parents, accepting the landscape where he lives, facing it; and then he can move.

BALDWIN: But what we are creating and have created means that people in this generation who did not grow up that way. . . .

You know, I have a friend who was born in Haiti in time to be thrown out and got to Algeria in time for the revolution and was thrown out of there and then went to France as a *pied-noir*—and in Marseilles that means you are treated like a dog—all this in a span of something like twenty or twenty-three years. He's never had a chance to figure out, which is perfectly typical of many millions of people, the landscape of his country. He's seen the blurred landscapes of three countries, but he's never had the experience of growing up with his own kind or even with his mother and his father. There was no mother, there was no father, there was no land. There was nothing. And this is perfectly typical of millions of people in this century.

MEAD: True, but you see the real problem is what are we going to do next? Where are we going to get some kind of anchorage within which people can move?

BALDWIN: Yes, but part of the problem is what is that particular kind of boy going to do? That particular kind of boy and that particular kind of girl? What has it made of him?

MEAD: Some of them are marvelous, you know.

BALDWIN: Some of them are, yes.

MEAD: And some of them are absolutely so uprooted and lost that they have very little left except hostility.

BALDWIN: And the hostile ones are, as usual, in the majority. Because it takes a lot to wrest identity out of nothing, and essentially that was the legacy.

MEAD: But nobody was talking about needing identity fifty

years ago. We've started to worry about identity since
people began losing it. And that gives us a new concept.
And now you go back and work on it and figure out what
your identity is. Fifty years ago you might have moved to
Paris because it was the thing to do. After all, lots of white
writers went to Europe too, in order to understand America. But you wouldn't have said the same things about
your identity fifty years ago.

BALDWIN: No, I suppose I wouldn't. In fact, I wouldn't have
had the time. And I wouldn't have lived long enough. I
was born nearly fifty years ago, but if I'd been a young
man fifty years ago my set of questions would have been,
perhaps, essentially the same one, but articulated very
differently. And I wouldn't have survived them—not
here.

MEAD: You don't think you would have survived them in the
North, in Harlem?

BALDWIN: I agree with Malcolm X, who said that if you're
south of the Canadian border you're South. You're born
in Harlem, but you don't grow up in Harlem saying: "Thank God I wasn't born in Atlanta." You've never
seen Atlanta, but you know what's happening to you in
Harlem, and Harlem is a dreadful place. It's a kind of
concentration camp, and not many people survive it. I
think the black people in this country are quite extraordinary. They must obviously have been the strongest people. To have survived that mid-passage, as you said much
earlier; to have survived those boats at all.

MEAD: And then to continue to survive.

BALDWIN: And to change, without the nation even knowing
it, to actually change something in the very deepest part
of the psychology of the nation. Because white people
cannot really live without black people here. Not any-

more. Not at all. And regardless of whether they act on it, they know and are in many ways unconsciously controlled by the fact that we are their brothers—not in the sense that all men are brothers, but in the literal sense of being related by blood.

MEAD: You see, I think that's a different point. It's absolutely true of the South, of course. I remember meeting a very prominent Negro educator who had been sent abroad by UNESCO. He'd been in some part of Europe for a couple of years, and he said, "It's so wonderful to get back to my country. I got so tired of all those white people over there. It's wonderful to come back where there are both black and white." And certainly for the Southern consciousness, black or white, both are there.

But the whole spirit of the North has been to keep other people out. It's not only been about keeping out black people, it's been about keeping out everybody. The Mayflower pact was itself a pact under which we were going to build our nice little society and keep everybody out. So the first thing you know you have Rhode Island, made up of refugees. The North has always tried to establish identity by cutting other people *out* and off.

BALDWIN: I agree. But if you're black it takes a very long time to realize that. It's only beginning. It's only now that black people in the main are beginning to recognize that many white people, if not most white people, are excluded from what Lyndon Johnson would have called the Great Society. The Great Society hasn't room for the poor-white West Virginian miner, for example. So obviously there's no room for me. This is part of the crisis, in fact: that it takes a long time before one can see that; that for a long time I simply knew that I was black and I was excluded because I was black. It didn't make any difference to me that the Irish were excluded, or that the Jews and the Poles were excluded. *I* was excluded and that was all that mattered to me. And furthermore, from a black American's vantage point—

MEAD: Also, remember that you're a Northerner.

BALDWIN: Well, in a way that doesn't mean anything to me.

MEAD: You are, though. You see you were shocked when you went south.

BALDWIN: Yes, I was shocked by the extent of the society's paranoia.

MEAD: You felt something strange and different. You are a Northerner. And one of the crises stems from the fact that there are many Northern black people who don't want other blacks around, especially black people from the South. You see, they're behaving like Northerners. So that in building any kind of an American society where we have to take into account the Southeast and take into account California and Old New England and all of this, we really have to take into account the way in which the Northern identity is dependent upon whom you can keep out.

BALDWIN: The American identity has always, from my point of view, depended on keeping me out.

MEAD: Yes, but not only you.

BALDWIN: As I said before, that perception comes later.

MEAD: Well, I'm perfectly willing to accept your point as it applies to a fifteen-year-old boy in Harlem. Nothing matters to him except his immediate life, and there is nothing you can offer him. If you offer him ten dollars to do a job he won't do the job, because there probably won't be another ten. There's no way for him to see that he will ever get anywhere.

BALDWIN: And he won't ever have any control over his own

destiny, which is the most demoralizing thing that there
is.

MEAD: It's horrible.

BALDWIN: It's the most terrible thing you can do to a person.

MEAD: So when we have this—and we not only have it in
Harlem, we also have it in Greenwich Village with white
boys—you go out and you offer them ten dollars to shovel
the snow from the front of your house and they won't
take it. Many people are shocked by this refusal. But I
know why they won't take it. I mean, what's ten dollars
unless you're an addict? If you're an addict you want ten
dollars now and you want another ten dollars in a few
hours. Otherwise, what's ten dollars? You're never, never,
never going to get where you've seen other people go. So
I'm not saying I don't understand your fifteen-year-old
boy a bit; I do understand him. But at the same time
we're going to have to build a country.

BALDWIN: We are going to have to do it according to prem-
ises which at this moment in this country are considered
absolutely treasonable. For a radical example, I agree
with the Black Panthers' position about black prisoners. I
think that one can make the absolutely blanket statement
that no black man has ever been tried by a jury of his
peers in America. And if that is so, and I know that is so,
no black man has ever received a fair trial in this country.
Therefore, I'm under no illusions about the reason why
many black people are in prison. I'm not saying there are
no black criminals. Still, I believe that all black prisoners
should be released and then retried according to principles more honorable and more just. Do you see what I
mean?

MEAD: Yes.

BALDWIN: But, of course, that is not about to happen next Wednesday, is it?

MEAD: I don't think so, no. Did you know that in many states you can't serve on a grand jury until you're over twenty-five?

BALDWIN: I didn't know that.

MEAD: So they're making the point that when you try an eighteen-year-old, he's not being tried by his peers. This was the case that has just been made in Wisconsin, where they actually have a law against his peers being on the jury. And, of course, no woman is ever tried by her peers.

BALDWIN: Yes, that's true.

MEAD: In fact, we don't do very well with peers. There aren't any peers in this country, except white middle-class Protestant men. They are the only people in the country who are not identified with a capital letter, though now they are talking about WASP and spelling it with capitals. You know, we have very, very slowly gotten to where we are. I mean, peers were sort of left over from the equality the barons of Runnymede forced from the English king. And we all had our hopes, but what we hoped for didn't really happen.

BALDWIN: No, it actually didn't happen in this country at all, did it?

MEAD: It moved along slowly, but after all it was a long time before we got rid of a poll tax, a long time before women got the right to vote, and now we are just going to give eighteen-year-olds the vote. We are moving pretty slowly compared with what we thought and with what we were told in school.

BALDWIN: Yes, compared with all that jazz.

MEAD: Now, I would like to go back to your fifteen-year-old boy. I can see perfectly clearly this fifteen-year-old boy standing on the street corner and only concerned with now. But the thing that I think at present is doing a lot of harm, both in this country and at international conferences, is the thing you were saying when you said, "I am concerned with my position." You see, you do not talk about American Indians except from your side of black, once in a while; that's sentimentality. You treat this country as if it had one problem. It has a lot more than one problem.

BALDWIN: Yes, but that one problem is a problem which has obsessed my life. And I have the feeling that that one problem, the problem of color in this country, has always contained the key to all the other problems. It is not an isolated, particular, peculiar problem. It is a symptom of all the problems in this country. And, in a way, this is indicated by the reaction in the country, and finally in the world, to the civil rights movement. Even the Women's Liberation Movement, you know, owes a lot to those people who started marching in Montgomery in 1956. And the whole black power movement in London comes from the United States. And the whole ferment which began in Montgomery when Mrs. Rosa Parks refused to stand up and give her seat to a white man, to give it an arbitrary date, has begun to overturn the entire country. And even the language in which people express their discontent, the language in which they fashion their petitions, comes out of the whole black confrontation in this country in the last fifteen to twenty years. If that is so, then you know that the problem—and I think the American Indian agrees with me—that the problem of the black and the Indian is related. In fact, the Puerto Ricans in the cities have taken techniques from the black rebellion. The Young Lords are a direct result of the Black Panthers.

MEAD: Of course.

BALDWIN: To me, that would seem to indicate that the key
to the salvation of America lies in whether or not it is able
to embrace the black face. If it cannot do that, I do not
think the country has a future.

MEAD: I don't think it's accurate to say it is the black face
alone. This is true of the South; there is no one down
there except black people and white people, and there
was never much immigration in the South, so it became a
biracial, tightly locked caste system. But in many other
parts of the country the issue has been different and has
worked. After all, you say it doesn't mean anything for
you to say what troubles the Irish went through or the
Italians, but it throws a lot of light on the country.

BALDWIN: I agree with that. But at the risk of being . . .
sounding a little fanatical, one has to . . . insist a little
on the importance of the black problem as a kind of
touchstone. Let me put it this way: Before, when I was
living in Europe, I could almost begin to judge a European by his attitude toward America. Now this may be a
terrible thing to say. It is very much like saying, for example, that when I was in California anybody driving around
with an American flag on his windshield or his bumper
was almost surely my enemy. Anyway, I distrusted Europeans who wanted to come to America. I had my fill of
seeing people come down the gangplank on Wednesday,
let us say, speaking not a word of English, and by Friday
discovering that I was working for them and they were
calling me nigger like everybody else. So that the Italian
adventure or even the Jewish adventure, however grim, is
distinguished from my own adventure, it seems to me, by
one thing. Not only am I black, but I am one of *our*
niggers. Americans can treat me in a certain way because

I am an American. They would never treat an African the way they treat me.

MEAD: Certainly, and if you learned French and could swear at them in French they would apologize.

BALDWIN: Once in Tallahassee, Florida—a very dreary, small anecdote, but very revealing to me—I was doing a story, and I was broke. I had been on the road for three months and I had run out of cash. Now, it is very frightening to be a vagrant in Tallahassee, Florida. Anyway, I got some money so I couldn't be put on the chain gang. But I had to go out and do a story; I just couldn't stay home while I was waiting for the money to come.

Finally the money came from my lawyer in New York, a certified bank check for only two hundred and fifty dollars. I got into a taxi with a black taxi driver, rushing to the bank to pick up this money. Now one of the things you have to go through in America is always saying to yourself, "Now, don't be paranoiac, Jimmy. Of course, they'll give me the money. It's my money." I asked the driver if he thought I'd have trouble cashing the check. He said, "I don't think they believe a nigger should have that much money." I thought, Oh, please, and got out of the cab at the bank. The driver said, "I'll wait for you. Bet you five dollars you don't get no money." I went into the bank. It was about five minutes before closing time and, no, they weren't going to give me the money that day. The taxi driver was right but he was very nice about it; he refused to take my five dollars.

I went back to the bank the next morning and two things happened, both of them revelations to me. I saw everybody in that bank before they would cash that check. I was determined that they were going to cash that check or lynch me. But, I was also curious about why I had to meet the president; I met *everybody,* and I ended up where I started. The teller who had to give me the money was a little white girl, needless to say. I gave her my passport; it was my only identification, which everyone at the bank had by now seen. And it is an American passport with the American eagle stamped all over it, and it says *U.S. Embassy* in great bright letters. She looked at the passport and looked at me with such a wonder that I suddenly began to see what I had done wrong. It is the first revelation. What I had done wrong was look her in the eye. I looked everybody in the eye, and black people in the deep South just do not look white people in the eye. That was the first thing. Then, when she looked at the passport, which had been issued in Paris, she looked at me with great relief. She said, "Oh, you're from Paris!" And this explained everything. Otherwise, she was in great trouble, because none of our niggers would behave like this. And that is really a terrifying comment on what we call the American way of life or the American sense of reality. The only way she could ever get it together, the only way she would understand that black boy in the bank, was to tell herself, "He doesn't know any better; he's from Paris." Otherwise she was going to be haunted to her dying day.

And that is what is happening in the country. All of a sudden the niggers, our niggers, are not acting like our niggers have always acted. And of course, they don't know that our niggers were never what they thought they were.

You know, a whole sublanguage and a subculture has been created in defense of black people by black people, because we have always known that white people could not in the generality be trusted. For example, when I was doing *Blues for Mister Charlie,* no white person had the remotest idea who Mr. Charlie was. Now "Mr. Charlie" is a phrase I have known all my life. I thought everybody knew it by this time. But no white person did. It was extraordinary to watch that. You sat outside of the theater and saw a black cat walking down the street—the marquee was up but the play was not open yet—and he would see the sign and he would pass the theater and then he would stop and look back as though to find out whether he'd seen what he thought he'd seen. Then he would walk back and look and really examine this, wondering what in the world a play called *Blues for Mister Charlie* was doing on Broadway. It's very sinister that nobody knows what Ray Charles is singing about.

MEAD: I think this is what you always have in these positions of disparate power. This is true of the Pygmies in Africa. For a long time the Pygmies in the Ituri Forest would have to come out and work for the big Negroes. People thought, These poor little creatures, they did not have any culture of their own and they just had to follow the ceremonies, have their children initiated by these people they worked for because they were just too little to have any culture vis-à-vis the big ones. And then when Colin Turnbull followed them back into the forest they just roared with laughter, because they had all their own ceremonies and their own music and their own language and everything.

Getting back to this treating your own worse than other people: Many men won't put up with from their wives what they will put up with from other women, because their wives are theirs and they are going to stay home and do what their husbands want. In Japan, a poor widow who came back to the house of her father or her brother was treated very badly. This treatment was part of his own

pride. It is a generalized human trait that you mistreat
your own people. I saw this happening in New Guinea. It
was fascinating, because in New Guinea, although race
was a factor, there was also this tremendous gap in culture, so that the people of New Guinea were treated like
natives, rather than in purely racial terms. The Australians
who came in didn't want to be there anyway; they got
New Guinea accidentally in World War I and then they
had to look after it. But those Australians have a very
large amount of white supremacy ideas.

BALDWIN: Oh, yes, I know. It's called the white man's country.

MEAD: Sure. When I was first in New Guinea, before World
War II, missionaries had come in to save their souls, but
there wasn't any kind of social equality. Natives stood up
in the presence of a European and they didn't chew betel
nut in the presence of a European and they called a European "Master" and so forth. Then Manus Island—the
archipelago only has fourteen thousand people in all—
was first taken by the Japanese and then it was taken by
the Americans in the battle of Los Negros. The Americans discovered that the fact they liked the Manus people
annoyed the Australians, so they put the Manus in the
chow line and treated them just like themselves and gave
them ice cream and pie like everybody else. The Australians were just tearing their hair, saying, "What is going
to happen after the war? How are we going to get these
people back into a proper position again?"

The Americans were primarily needling the Australians. However, in this situation they were perfectly
willing to indulge the Manus and enjoy them and treat
them like people. Meanwhile, the Manus saw black
American troops. Now, at this point the black troops were

still in work battalions, but from the Manus' point of view they had all the big bulldozers and all the other big machinery, so they thought the Americans had made "the man of Africa all right." He spoke the same language, he wore the same clothes and ate the same food. So from these two things, neither one of them something to hold up as a great model, the Manus got the idea that they were human beings also, and that they could do anything the white man could do. So from being people who were caught in the stereotype that they were natives and could never be anything *but* natives—that they could learn a little of this and a little of that, but they still would stay natives who could not travel from their own village without a passport and who worked for the white man for two pounds a month—they suddenly got the idea that they were people.

Next they devised their own version of Christianity. They were people who had no figures of speech at all. Originally, they said, Jesus had talked in perfectly clear language, but those pharisees who wanted to keep religion secret had made up figures of speech and hidden things so that it was not very clear anymore. And when they came to New Guinea, they divided Christianity up and gave some to the Catholics and some to Protestants, different groups of Protestants, and again people could not get at the truth.

Well, according to their version, time went on and the Lord looked at the world and the only country that wasn't doing well was New Guinea. So first he sent the English, and they did not do very well. Then he sent the Germans, and they didn't do very well. Then he sent the Americans, and they were all right except they wouldn't stay; they went home. Then the Lord said that there was just nothing to do but try the people of New Guinea themselves.

BALDWIN: That is fabulous! That's fabulous!

MEAD: Therefore, they stood up and they devised their own society, and they skipped two thousand years in twenty-five.

BALDWIN: That is fabulous. It makes perfect sense, too. There is something in that about the way in which the world's work actually gets done. It relates to that whole business of not being sentimental. It makes perfect sense to me; I can see what they saw, you know. I wonder what my brother would have seen or what I would have seen had we been in the work battalion. But that is less important ultimately, isn't it? It may be that America will end up, quite against its will, proving to other people something about freedom which Americans themselves may not believe.

MEAD: Quite. Because, you see, they said, "We learned from America that the only thing that matters are human beings. That *things* do not matter at all."

BALDWIN: That is a very paradoxical lesson to learn from Americans.

MEAD: They were looking at the G.I.s handling government property, and they were so generous. They gave the Manus the most beautiful sets of tools you ever saw, and all sorts of other things.

BALDWIN: And Americans are generous.

MEAD: Especially with government property. And they are generous in general. So they saw all the paraphernalia of a base hospital, and—

BALDWIN: All that has happened in the twentieth century, and black people, as far as they could tell, had control of it.

MEAD: So they saw all this being expended to send one wounded man home. This *tremendous* expenditure. But then they added, "You see, the reason Americans don't care about things is because they have plenty of them."

BALDWIN: A perfectly sound observation.

MEAD: They said to me, "Now look, you remember"—because I was there in 1928—"you remember how our pots broke. They were very thin, very brittle. We had to beat a child who broke a pot like that. You remember when you went away you gave Markarita"—who was a baby who was named after me while I was there—"a great big iron pot which is still here. When we can get good things that won't break, we don't have to beat our children."

BALDWIN: What you realize is that one makes very funny assumptions, and it's unconscious. There was a day in my life, after all, when I did not know what that lamp over there is. One day I saw a lamp for the first time like everybody else and learned the difference between that electric lamp, which sometimes would go on and sometimes not, and the kerosene lamps we would have to use in Harlem, years ago. What I am trying to get at is that once people know what they know, they make the unconscious assumption that they were *born* knowing what they know, and forget that they had to *learn* everything they know. They learned it from example and then learned it being around it. I would never be able to put together a motor of an automobile, for example, because I have never been related to automobiles in any way whatever. It is as great a mystery to me as sending a rocket to the moon. So one has got to realize that the world is full of people who have never seen a rocket or who have never seen an electric lamp.

Once I found myself in a tent in the desert in Israel, in

the middle of absolutely nowhere, and the only thing in
that tent, apart from the sheik's fifty-seven sons, was a
television set. It blew my mind completely. Everybody
was there sitting in front of this . . . this miracle; it was
for them. Now, I can't bear television sets. But I can
afford not to bear them because I read books. For me it is
just another invention.

Now whether I like it or not, no matter what my attitude is toward America, or toward the Western world, it
is still true that I was born in it. And because I had to
learn certain skills before I learned anything else, the
price may have been higher than other people can imagine. But that, after all, concerned *me* at the moment and
not them. The point is that it is a *fait accompli,* and
whether America likes it or not, it has produced—

MEAD: It did produce you.

BALDWIN: Yes, it did, and you hear this everywhere in the
world. When my brother David and I were in London,
David had a small argument with a black Englishman and
David said something which at first sight seems very trivial, and yet, when you think about it, it is very important.
For years and years and years black Englishmen have put
down black Americans and West Indians. When I was
young, they despised black Americans and West Indians
because they, black Englishmen, had never been slaves.
Now David said, "I don't care if all that is true. I come to
London and I don't hear your island songs. I go to Stockholm and I don't hear your island songs. But no matter
where I go in the world, I hear Aretha Franklin."

I thought to myself years ago, It is a very good thing
that I didn't try to escape from my roots because I would
now be in terrible trouble, since there is no place I can go
where the music will not follow me. And that says some-

thing very important. What boys and girls in Stockholm are trying to get related to and what boys and girls in Africa are trying to get related to has something to do with some experience out of which that music comes, some kind of instinctive knowledge that what the blacks in the West have had to learn they will have to learn, too. They will have to go through the same fire, no matter what the fire is like behind them, the fire of being a black Westerner; and there is no option; one's got to go through it. That is the coming ordeal. Of course, since I am at bottom an optimist, I think this necessity, and this journey and this ordeal, is precisely where the hope of the West lies, that this in fact will change, has to change, the Western assumptions, and make it a larger civilization than it has ever been before. Do you see what I mean?

MEAD: I don't think there is any doubt that the domination of the white world over the rest of the world is a short accident of history. You always write as if you thought these whites have been ruling the world forever, but they have only been ruling it a rather short time. It is a very new, upstart civilization that happened to develop a technology that could go around the world.

I remember a friend of mine writing from Chungking in World War II, and he said, "This is the last peace the white man is ever going to write, and he had better make it good." But the thing I worry about is proportion. I sit down in a group of fifteen or twenty people of every nationality—Indians, Koreans, Japanese, Dutch, French, English, Americans—and if there are any really lively black Americans there, they take over. They speak for everybody, they push everybody down, especially the Indians, and they are the only people that matter. Now this is, of course, very American.

BALDWIN: It is, indeed, very American. But I can tell you something about that because I have been in that situation. I can tell you something about it because—how can I put this?—at the risk of sounding arrogant, and I am not speaking exactly in my own person right now, my experience, historically, has been extraordinary. And a black American who finds himself outside of this setting, confronting an Indian, if you like, or an African, is of all in a kind of psychological trouble. You see, on one level you are obviously brothers, and on another level you are equally obviously estranged.

When I first hit Paris, for example, I had dealt with cynical East and North Africans. They did not see me, and it may be argued that I did not see them either. But they did see that I smoked Lucky Strikes and Pall Malls and that I had American sports shirts. They did not see that I did not have a penny; that did not make any difference. I came, I represented the richest nation in the world and there was no way whatever for them to suspect that I considered myself to be far worse off than they. . . . The reason I was in Paris was that I considered my sports shirts, for example, and my cigarettes, had been a little too expensive and cost me a little more than I could afford. They did not know that. Now, it took a long time before we began to understand each other, and one of the fires we had to pass through—and this is what happened in one of the meetings we were discussing—is the sometimes instinctive reaction of a darker brother who is not a Westerner to attack you.

I remember once a few years ago, in the British Museum, a black Jamaican was washing the floors or something and asked me where I was from, and I said I was born in New York. He said, "Yes, but where are you from?" I did not know what he meant. "Where did you come from before that?" he explained. I said, "My mother was born in Maryland." "Where was your father born?" he asked. "My father was born in New Orleans." He said, "Yes, but where are you from?" Then I began to get it; very dimly, because now I was lost. And he said, "Where are you from in Africa?" I said, "Well, I don't know," and he was furious with me. He said, and walked away, "You mean you did not care enough to find out?"

Now, how in the world am I going to explain to him that there is virtually no way for me to have found out where I come from in Africa? So it is a kind of tug of war. The black American is looked down on by other dark people as being an object abjectly used. They envy him on one hand, but on the other hand they also would like to look down on him as having struck a despicable bargain. Therefore the black American had to sometimes sound a little crushing to let these people know that he paid a very high price for whatever it is they think he has, and that they are going to have to pay a terribly high price, too. And that we are going to have to learn from each other or else we will both be destroyed. It is very hard to explain to a black Englishman in London what it is like to be born in Harlem, because he still thinks that he is English and it is going to take another generation before he realizes that he is not. It is going to take another generation before the African people become independent of Europe, and European history, *in their minds*.

MEAD: You mean English-speaking Africans? You're not talking of someone from Liverpool?

BALDWIN: No, I mean someone who has just come to London from—

MEAD: Nigeria?

BALDWIN: Nigeria, for example.

MEAD: Or Ghana, or something of that sort?

BALDWIN: Yes. Somebody born in Liverpool is quite another
case, something different altogether. But there are comparatively very few black people, by comparison to the
American black situation, born in Liverpool.

MEAD: They are very interesting though. You know, they
couldn't dance.

BALDWIN: I met some of them. They can't dance?

MEAD: No, you see they have white mothers. They had
white lower-class mothers who were just sort of cold potatoes; their African fathers were sailors and didn't stay at
all. When our troops got to England in World War II, of
course everyone thought it so nice for the black American
troops to associate with the colored people in Liverpool—
not one of whom had a secondary school education, by
the way. But the thing that really riled the black American was they couldn't dance! I mean, what in thunder are
you doing with black people who can't dance? And of
course they also were furious. In World War I the first
American black troops had found black troops speaking
French. If black people couldn't speak English it was too
much.

BALDWIN: Yes, this happens until today when the Puerto Ricans—

MEAD: And if you really look at this, you see, it is very
American; it's extraordinarily American.

BALDWIN: Of course it is, of course it is.

MEAD: And, of course, I shouldn't complain about the
bumptiousness of black Americans because it is exactly
like the bumptiousness of white Americans.

BALDWIN: I'll say this, though, of black Americans, at the
risk of sounding chauvinistic, and even knowing what I

know. I watched them now for twenty years. I watched
black Americans abroad, and on balance I really have to
give the black man a kind of accolade in spite of all his
hang-ups and all his pretensions. More often than it happens with white people, a black American will find himself in Milan or in Rome or in Turkey and will really be
curious about the people. Most white Americans travel in
a kind of plastic case designed to prevent anything from
ever happening to them, a kind of magic plastic case out
of which they produce—

MEAD: Fried eggs and American bacon.

BALDWIN: —fried eggs and bacon and good American coffee. But a black American will very often, more often than
a white American—and I don't say always—really try to
find out what is happening with the people and be curious
and try this, and that, and even drink something awful
tasting. He will, really, and you know the people respond
to him differently than they respond to white Americans.

When I was living in Istanbul, for example, I really,
without quite realizing it, became a great threat to the
American colony there, partly because the American government is always taking the extraordinary position that I
just don't exist. I was one of the very few black things in
Istanbul, except for various soldiers and sailors, and certainly the most famous black American there. But the
American government just thought it was simpler to ignore me. Well, what happened was this attracted the
wondering attention of the Turks. I didn't care; I didn't
want to be dragged to any of those ghastly embassy parties. It didn't make any difference to me at all, but it
made a great difference to the Turks. It taught them
something about the Americans, in a rather awful way. A
student walked into my house one afternoon, for example,

and asked me—this is the first time I realized what was happening—"Why are you on a blacklist," I did not know I was on a blacklist, but when she asked me that I realized that the students knew I was in town and had been asking their teachers why I could not come and speak to them.

What I am trying to get at is that the American terror of the world, of reality, the American attempt to deny and manipulate experience, I have always equated with the American terror of dealing with me as a human being, dealing with Sambo. I have watched it all over the world now—the way Americans treat other people. They are just as afraid of the Greeks and Turks and the Japanese, and even the French, as they are of me. What I am saying is that the American sense of reality and the American sense of the world has been somehow hopelessly inhibited by the attempt to get away from something which is really theirs. You know, I really belong to them and they really belong to me. And the level of human experience which they have always denied has had a disastrous effect on their sense of what is going on around them.

They don't understand the Turks when the Turks hit the streets any more than they understood Birmingham when the blacks there hit the streets. They do not know yet how it is that the Japanese students were able to prevent Eisenhower from landing in Japan. They don't know why, a few months ago, Turkish students lined up on the Bosporus and forbade the Sixth Fleet to enter, drove them out. The Americans don't know why, but I know why.

MEAD: Yes, I see what you mean. But we are really in a sense talking about two different things here. I am talking about the functioning of black Americans in international conferences and committees and the way they take over to a degree, not someone who lives abroad. Now I can remember twenty-five years ago, on a committee, if we had—and, you know, it is an anachronism to say black American—if we had Negro Americans on that committee, they took enormous responsibilities. They usually could see both sides of what was going on; they were very patient and they were very, very constructive. And, you could count on them as being the people who had more insight than other people and who did seem, in a sense, to be rather like the guardians of a greater democracy. But this is quite different from taking over and speaking for everybody, you see.

BALDWIN: Oh, I agree with that.

MEAD: And deciding for Japan, China, Korea, India, the works.

BALDWIN: That is a kind of sentimental bombast which—

MEAD: Yes, but it is what Americans do too.

BALDWIN: Americans do it. Americans do it with even less authority.

MEAD: I think one of the very important things you have done is to keep on saying that, after all, you are an American.

BALDWIN: Well, I'm not anything else. I discovered I was an American when I got off the boat in France. I was an American at the age of twenty-four, for the very first time in my life. I became an American in a foreign country because I was not anything else. It was not, I mean, a matter for rejoicing. It was a great shock. It was a tremendous, tremendous revelation. I became an American at twenty-four, and I realized what it meant, both for better and for worse. That experience—and again I am speaking not exactly in my own person—really says something of utmost importance about the moral life of the West, again for better and for worse: the fact that I had to leave my country in order to realize that I was a part of it, or that it was a part of me.

The whole question, for example, of religion has always really obsessed me. I was raised in the church and I left it when I was seventeen and never joined anything else again, not even a riding academy. Nothing. But I never understood white Christians. I still don't. I remember the photographs of white women in New Orleans, several years ago, during the school integration crisis, who were standing with their babies in their arms, and in the name of Jesus Christ they were spitting on other women's children, women who happened to be black, women with *their* babies in their arms. I have never been able to understand that at all. To put it in rather exaggerated primitive terms, I don't understand at all what the white man's religion means to him. I know what the white man's religion has done to *me*. And so, I could—can—accuse the white Christian world of being nothing but a tissue of lies, nothing but an excuse for power, as being as removed as anything can possibly be from any sense of worship and, still more, from any sense of love. I cannot understand that religion. And I really mean that. I am not joking when I say I cannot understand it. I mean, I can have a fight with a bartender or I can have a fight with you, I think, but I can't have a fight with a baby, with a child.

There is a photograph from the Second World War which is haunting my memory—stays in my memory forever. It's of a little Jewish boy about five or six, and by the time I saw this photograph he was dead. The Gestapo had just surrounded him. He was standing in a street looking down at his shoes: a beautiful little boy, and he looked the way little boys look when they've peed on themselves.

You know, he just did not know what had happened to him. And they were going to take that little boy away and kill him because he was a Jew. And this is in the name of Christianity! I know that human beings do this all the time, but I never understood it.

MEAD: I don't believe you can say the Nazis did it in the name of Christianity.

BALDWIN: The first European power to sign a concordat with Hitler was the pope. And I am old enough to remember the Italian-Ethiopian war, when the pope of that church which stands in Rome sent out white Italian boys with his blessing to rape Ethiopia.

MEAD: They also used to bless the Germans when they were going to rape the French, and the French when they were going to rape the Germans. You are dealing with a period where people blessed every army.

BALDWIN: What I am dealing with is the morality beneath all this.

MEAD: But you also have to ask, "Where do you get *your* conception of morality?"

BALDWIN: I get my conception of morality from—from the way I watched. . . . I get it partly from . . . where indeed do I get it?

MEAD: Where do you get it?

BALDWIN: That is a good question.

MEAD: You see!

BALDWIN: I don't get it from the Bible.

MEAD: Not from the Bible but from Christianity. After all, where do we get our evaluation of children?

BALDWIN: I have known a few Christians. The first Christian I knew was my mother. I understood a lot about what she was doing to all the children, which cost us a great deal, but it saved us too. Somehow she really made us believe it was more important for us to love each other and love other people than anything else.

MEAD: Yes, where did you get that?

BALDWIN: We got it from her. I did not get it from any preacher. I did not get it from any church.

MEAD: Yes, but this is just an anti-establishment remark.

BALDWIN: No, I was a preacher for three and a half years.

MEAD: But you gave it up. I think you have to look at part of the Western tradition out of which what conscience it has —out of which the impetus toward peace and brotherhood and all of these things have come. They *have* come out of the ideas of Christianity. We took them to India and we took them to Japan—

BALDWIN: But what I insist on is that these ideas, in respect to the lives of black Americans or to all the great unwashed, have always been betrayed. Insofar as I can be called a Christian, I became a Christian by not imitating white people. Of course, that is a blanket statement, because there are obviously white exceptions. But if I had tried to become a Christian by imitating what the Christians did, I would be dead, or a monster.

MEAD: But you could imitate what your mother did.

BALDWIN: Yes, yes, I had to. I had to do that because I loved my brothers and my sisters and I loved her, and we all had to depend on each other. That was a very private necessity, or responsibility. I know what you are getting at: In the long view that is also part of an historical process. But what Christians seem not to do is identify themselves with the man they call their Savior, who, after all, was a very disreputable person when he was alive and who was put to death by Rome, helped along by the Jews in power under Rome. And everyone forgets that.

So, in my case, in order to become a moral human

being, whatever that may be, I have to hang out with publicans and sinners, whores and junkies, and stay out of the temple where they told us nothing but lies anyway.

MEAD: This is, of course, what Jesus did too.

BALDWIN: Yes, but it is only in that sense that I can be called a Christian.

MEAD: I am not trying to call you a Christian. What I am talking about is that one gets from the Christian tradition—

BALDWIN: I'll accept the term because I am not a Muslim.

MEAD: —everything. That the good things that we have, the good things you are insisting on—that people should love each other and recognize each other as brothers—is a Christian idea.

BALDWIN: But it isn't only a Christian idea. Isn't it also a Muslim idea?

MEAD: No. Because Muslims don't believe in loving everybody as brothers. They only love Muslims as brothers. They don't really have an idea of universal brotherhood.

BALDWIN: Yeah, all right. I'll accept that, because I'm not equipped to argue it.

MEAD: And you can find it in Buddhism, but you didn't get it from Buddhists. Now, that's the point. You and I, what we have in the belief in the brotherhood of man, of all men, or the power of love, we got out of the Christian tradition.

BALDWIN: Did we? I mean, I accept the premise. I know what you are saying. But at the risk of being difficult, did we? I wonder. It seems to me that there are lots of ways to read the New Testament, and in my experience no pope, except perhaps John XXIII, can possibly have read it.

MEAD: Well, when they elected John XXIII they suddenly

elected a Christian pope. I mean, it's a very odd thing
for—

BALDWIN: It's a very odd thing for Christians to do. That's
my point. What are those people then to be considered in
the New Orleans parish? I don't want to belabor them,
but I cannot claim to have gotten anything from them
except the opposite lessons. What I am trying to get at is
if any particular discipline—whether it be Christianity,
Buddhism or LSD, God forbid—does not become a matter of your personal honor, your private convictions, then
it's simply a cloak which you can wear or throw off. If it is
not interiorized, as we would say these days, then it really
is meaningless, and in that sense, it seems to me, the
Christian church is meaningless. The *Christian church* as
church.

MEAD: Well, you know the great thing about a church is
that it can breed heresies, whereas the sects can't.

BALDWIN: Yes, that may be true, that may be true. Still, if I
were a white Christian I'd be in great psychological or
spiritual trouble. However, I've known some white Christians—I mean real ones. I don't mean this quite the way it
sounds; I don't mean that they are as rare as all that. But
the ones I've known were always in trouble. The last one I
knew well had to leave the church in order to do what he
felt he had to do. And what he was doing was very simple
and important: He was simply working with young kids in
settlement houses up and down Manhattan—blacks and
Puerto Ricans, some of whom were junkies. He was doing
what he could to rehabilitate—in fact, to love—those children. The parish priest disapproved and kicked him out.

Of course, that is a very trivial anecdote, but it's the
same way the American government performed in Turkey. And that performance is something the Turks will

remember and we'll forget, just as the church's performance in that ghetto parish is something the children will remember and the priest may forget.

Of course, I can also see that this gap between profession and performance can be very illuminating and have great effect, so that this is one of the ways in which the world changes. I am not being as vehemently romantic and sentimental as I may sound. I think I understand that, or I am beginning to understand that. Yet it still seems to me a terrible crime to profess one thing and do another.

MEAD: Some psychologists were doing a study somewhere, and they asked the little white boys which they would rather be, little white girls or little Negro boys. What do you think they said?

BALDWIN: I can't guess.

MEAD: They said they would rather be little Negro boys.

BALDWIN: Ha, that's encouraging. They had some sanity left.

MEAD: Well, you define people as human and nonhuman in certain sorts of terms, and this is the kind of behavior you get. But when you consider that twenty thousand years ago people weren't capable of thinking of more than thirty or forty people as human. And the people on the next hill were either people that were going to hunt them or people they could hunt. And if you incorporate someone else's lower status as an element in who you are, then you are really trapped.

You know, men do that about women, and they are unmanned because a woman gets a job of the sort they are doing. The American Army, for instance, fought tooth and nail against women doctors who, they claimed, would completely wreck the Army. The Faculty of Political Science at Columbia fought tooth and nail against having a woman professor. American men become absolutely vulnerable, because what most American men have been taught is that the point of being a man is that you're not a woman.

BALDWIN: Which is exactly not the point.

MEAD: It certainly is not the point.

BALDWIN: The point of being a man is being a man.

MEAD: In the South an essential element in the identity of each race was they weren't the other. So if you change the position of the member of the other race you're threatening the other person's identity.

BALDWIN: That's what's happening now. With religion and everything else that we think of as crutches and used to think of as bulwarks, the opposites are used to protect your identity. What is sinister is that, when one's identity is so profoundly threatened, statecraft and religion become only weapons to defend your identity. In South Africa that is obviously what is happening. That is what the late Verwoerd meant when he said, "God is on our side." Then something very serious is happening to our civilization, or Western civilization, because it no longer believes in its avowed first principles but is merely acting out of panic.

MEAD: You see, I don't think we can really make the old analogies about a particular civilization. I think what we are moving toward is world civilization, only it isn't born yet.

BALDWIN: Well, that's the only hope the world has. But the difficulty with it is that it won't be born without several midwives, some of whom we have to create.

MEAD: Yes, that's right. Now we have to go back to the bomb for a minute, and your statement of why this fifteen-year-old boy should be angry. The bomb has given us our first chance of a world peace.

BALDWIN: Yes, I quite agree with that. In fact, history is not
sentimental either, as it turns out, any more than nature
is, and the way things get done is really quite terrifying.
You have to accept that. And I know it is difficult to accept that it took the lives of all those millions of people to
cause mankind to suspect—they do not yet fully realize it
—that their principal achievement so far has been the
ability to destroy themselves. Yet that suspicion means
that war is obsolete.

MEAD: I am not willing to say that our principal achievement so far is our ability to destroy ourselves. I think we
have a few other little achievements around.

BALDWIN: Perhaps. But that is the most glaring one. Let us
put it that way. And, of course, I am speaking again—you
must understand this—I am speaking essentially as one of
those most betrayed by the West. However Western I
may be, I am also, as I said before, the despised bastard
of the Western house. So I am also speaking from the
point of view of someone who has been told that this is
the greatest civilization the world has ever seen, while
looking at it from my vantage point. I can have a lot of
other things to say about it. I am not so sure that I would
really want to become the epitome of an Englishman, and
still less a white American. I don't agree that this is something *I* want. It is still less something I want for my heirs.
If I thought that my only option was to turn into Richard
Nixon, Spiro Agnew, Ronald Reagan or Governor Wal-
lace or any of these representatives of Western civilization, I would much rather get a few more bottles of
Scotch and twenty-seven sleeping pills and a razor and
give the whole thing up.

MEAD: But you're not going to give it up.

BALDWIN: Oh, I can't give it up. Luckily, I'm not—I don't

think I am—in danger of becoming Mr. Reagan or Mr. Wayne. But if I thought I were! And to be told that these are the people who are the sum of the Western glory! If this is the standard to which one is expected to aspire, that impresses me as an insult to the human race, not merely to myself, not merely to black people.

You see, what I am trying to get at, too, is that whether I am always rational or not is not as important a question as I used to think it was. I would like to think of myself as being an exceedingly rational human being. However, trying to think of myself as rational is what gives me my sense of humor. What is important, and one of the elements that makes history, is the reaction of human beings to their situation. And that reaction, when it is a real reaction, is always excessive and always a little blind. You simply find your situation intolerable and you set about to change it, and when you do that, you place yourself in a certain kind of danger: the danger of being excessive, the danger of being wrong. That is the only way you ever learn anything, and it is also the only way the situation ever changes. One has to deal with that, too.

I may have reservations about . . . oh, let's say Huey Newton, because I love Huey and I don't mind using him this way. I may not agree with everything Huey says. I may not think that Huey is always right, but I know what he means and I know that he is learning all the time. I know that he means it. And that he can listen. And I know that if I were twenty-seven or twenty-eight—when I was twenty-seven or twenty-eight—*my* situation, the situation objectively, was different and in many ways much worse, partly because someone like Huey was scarcely a possibility then. All black people want to live. The black man, or boy, begins to lash out. He begins to fight and he really has to prepare himself to die, because you cannot accept going through the world covered with white people's spit. Huey did it one way, I did it another, and no doubt we both made our terrible mistakes. But that is the only way. You've got to tell the world how to treat you. If the world tells you how you are going to be treated, you are in trouble. That's part of what is happening.

MEAD: That's what is happening.

BALDWIN: I don't agree with all of these people running around with Afro wigs. And God knows I'm tired of being *told*, by people who just got out of the various white colleges and got a dashiki and let their hair grow; I am terribly tired of these middle-class darkies telling me what it means to be black. But I *understand* why they have to do it!

MEAD: It is really the poor middle-class white man who is having a terrible time too. First he had the white boys that let their hair grow and made them look like girls, and that upset him. Then he gets the Afro haircut where the hair stands straight up on the head and is threatening and nothing on earth—

BALDWIN: Makes them all look like boys.

MEAD: . . . all these black boys, so that he has had it from both sides. It is really rough.

BALDWIN: It is rough indeed. But they brought it, to be merciless, on themselves. And I know that they couldn't help it.

MEAD: Well, who had brought it on themselves, Cromwell's men when they cut off their hair?

BALDWIN: No, I see your point. But when I say they brought it on themselves, I am deliberately taking a very narrow view. And I have to do it that way because, for the moment, I know one thing. I am forty-six, okay? Whatever has happened to me has happened to me and that's all right; it doesn't make any difference now. But I have a great-nephew who is two years old, and he is not going to live the life I have had to live. If it demands blowing up the Empire State Building, or whatever it demands, I will not be a party to it twice.

In a sense that's my real frame of reference. I know exactly what you mean and I agree with it. But that two-year-old kid, though I know he is an historical figure, is not an historical figure for me. I have to give him whatever it is I can give him. I don't believe that the band of mediocrities which appear to rule this country now have any right whatever to tell him where to sit and where to stand and who he is and what he is going to become. And I won't let them do it. Really, it is as simple as that.

August 27th...10 A.M.

MEAD: I have been reading all this stuff this morning about Women's Lib and also letters to me from people who have nice communes—they say. And you know, we are now going to have the end of white supremacy, male chauvinism and a few other things like that.

BALDWIN: No doubt, yes.

MEAD: Now, it seemed to me that if we could take what you said about the tremendous contribution that is possible for black people who have grown up in the new world. . . . You really have to include the Caribbean and people there who speak either English or French as their native language, don't you? I mean, they don't have any other language either. So that either English, French or Spanish—

BALDWIN: Yes, that's true, but I always—

MEAD: You don't feel they have the same access?

BALDWIN: Well, I don't know. I really don't know. I hesitate to speak about them because there is one distinction between their situation and mine, and it is simply that they live with each other. Do you see what I mean?

MEAD: Yes. And on little islands.

BALDWIN: And on little islands. And I suspect that makes a vast difference in the way one looks at the world and to one's psychology. Because it is one thing to be speaking English in Manhattan among white people—and one way or another adjusting or reacting to white people—and another thing living on an island, living in and out of the water, speaking whatever language they speak, but speaking it to people who look like themselves. In other words, it is not a question of their access—

MEAD: To the language, but to the rest of society.

BALDWIN: But to the rest of society. And I think they bring another attitude toward it which is not at all in any way meant to be any kind of value judgment.

MEAD: That is different. But I think if you are going to make your widest point, the special role of people who have, as a first language, a European language, have a different role than those whose first language is Chinese.

BALDWIN: Or Arabic.

MEAD: Or Arabic or Indian. People who have either French or English, particularly—and if they had German or Russian it would be true—have a special mediating role in the present day world.

BALDWIN: I agree with that. I think that one of the things that's beginning to happen is that American black people

and the people in the Caribbean, for example, are beginning to recognize to what extent they need each other.
They have begun almost instinctively to work out the
terms of their connection. Because neither they nor I can
turn to England or France or America for some very essential things which only we know about and can supply
for each other.

MEAD: And, of course, they have in the Caribbean just what
you have here: They have a language they speak to each
other that no one else can understand.

BALDWIN: That no one can penetrate.

MEAD: Now, there are some white people in the British
islands who can speak it. I mean, they grew up there. As
children they learned it and they understand it and they
can even speak it. But you have to have really lived with
the people to speak it. And then they shift. I have listened
to them. I have a colleague who has worked in Montser-
rat, and I have watched her start doing interviews when I
was present—and I don't speak both the languages—
starting in standard English, which, of course, they speak
perfectly well; and then slowly, as everything was going
better, they went further and further and further back
into their own dialect.

BALDWIN: Inevitably. And this happens in West Africa
where they speak—I can't speak it but my sister learned it
—creole, which is a kind of patois made up of, God
knows, odds and ends of English but a very odd English,
indeed. It is as though you are speaking an African dialect
in English.

MEAD: Yes. It probably has the grammar of an African language, or the vocabulary. Well, you see, that is the kind of
language I speak in New Guinea, too. I learned the peo-

ple's own languages, and there we have seven hundred languages among—

BALDWIN: Seven hundred different languages?

MEAD: Among two million people.

BALDWIN: Jesus Christ!

MEAD: Six hundred people speaking a language. But there also is a lingua franca there which we used to call pidgin English, and which we now call Neo-Melanesian. I have been fighting for that language. And it is going to be a language, because now within the ecumenical movement the New Testament is being translated into it. So it is being saved. Otherwise, all the rows about slave languages and vernaculars that came up in the United Nations were going to kill it, and it is the only possible language to start in for people who come from seven hundred different languages.

You can't ask teachers to learn them. I speak it just as well as any New Guinea native. I'll never speak his mother tongue as well, and he'll never speak English as well as I do, but we can both speak Neo-Melanesian to each other. I can swear in it and I can talk a mile a minute. I can talk it in its bush version that the average white person can't understand, and I can talk the kind that the white man talks in town when he has anglicized all the words that sound remotely like English.

And then we have real communication, because the only—it seems to me that the time you have real communication is when two people speak the language as well or as badly as each other. You see, when you have two French-speaking people, neither of whom have French as their mother tongue, they can communicate with each other beautifully in bad French. Do you agree with me?

BALDWIN: Yes, I agree with that. I think that the history of

the English-American language, let's say English-Ameri-
can-Black language, is a history of an extraordinary kind
of transition: a transition from what you once called the
King's English, to what happened when people left England and came here, to what happened when slaves began to communicate with each other and to what happened when slaves began to communicate with their
masters, to what is happening now. It is a kind of extraordinary study, because there are some things even today
that Americans can say to each other that no one else
understands. And I mean perfectly ordinary Americans,
black and white. Americans in England talking to each
other are really speaking a foreign language.

MEAD: And if the English try to read American poetry
aloud—

BALDWIN: Yes, oh, God!

MEAD: But we can still read English poetry aloud. It's a
one-way street.

BALDWIN: Yes. That proves something, doesn't it? It's very
funny. I can read Shakespeare, but they have trouble with
Whitman.

MEAD: Because they stay at the center of the language, at
what as we still call it, is English. So you and I go back to
it.

BALDWIN: We go back to it almost as reference, almost like
looking up a word, almost like checking theologies.

MEAD: They never come out to us. They just sit down at the
center and stay there.

BALDWIN: I suppose they don't because they don't have to.

MEAD: Their language is their mother tongue. Of course, if
you look at England in detail, when you get up to York-
shire or near there you have a language—

BALDWIN: That's something else again. Isn't it? Even in Liverpool?

MEAD: Oh, certainly in Liverpool. Now, what I would like to ask you, because it worries me: about all the discussions that have been going on here, in this country about black English. We started saying that there is a form of English that is spoken by blacks among themselves which is a different dialect than, say, the dialect spoken by mountain whites or the dialect that is spoken in Maine. But a great many black leaders were angry about this, and one reason they were angry is that Americans tend to call everything except standard English "bad English" or "bad grammar" and don't recognize the vitality of all of these regional languages. But I think the move in this country was a good one, to insist that teachers, if they are going to be teachers for black Americans, working with little children, ought to learn to understand the language the children speak. Then they can go ahead with standard English if they want to, but they ought to be asked to learn the black English. I think we also ought to be able to recognize the far greater dependence of black people on the ear, which I don't think is genetic but has been a direct, continuous inheritance from Africa. Do you agree with that?

BALDWIN: I think so, if what you're getting at is that the African sense of history is radically different from the European sense of history. I mean, for a very long time it would have appeared that the Africans had no sense of history because—

MEAD: They didn't have anything written down.

BALDWIN: —because it had not been written down. But now it occurs to me—especially when I try, without any equipment at all, to guess how it happened—that for nearly four hundred years something within me has been handed down. I mean, James Baldwin, sitting here, is still not only visibly, physically, recognizably of African origin, but something in me has been handed down to me.

MEAD: Right straight down.

BALDWIN: Yes. Now, how it was handed down is a mystery, but I begin to think that part of it is that the African sense of reality seems to be so radically different from the European because it involves containing. Someone once said to me that the African sense of art was involved not with the eternality of the thing produced—the painting, or the sculpture, or whatever artifact it was—but with an attempt to trap the energy or the—

MEAD: Essence of something.

BALDWIN: The essence of something. So that it did not make any difference if the vase was broken or the painting disappeared, because it could be created again—trapping the essence of something. I think that the African sense of history has something to do with that, in the sense that everyone becomes a kind of receptacle of that history.

MEAD: I agree with you. Also, Africans have a tremendous capacity to deal with what we technically call now an oral tradition or oral history. So that when writing came along it did not represent to them what it had represented, for instance, to the peoples of the South Seas. When I arrived among the Manus they had already been quarreling for thousands of years about how many dog's teeth somebody paid to somebody else. They could count up in the thousands in their heads, but of course you couldn't prove what was in somebody else's head, so it was an endless quarrel. So the first thing they said when I came along was "Ah, now, Piyap"—that's what they called me—Woman of the West—"can write it down. You write down every single transaction and we won't need to quarrel anymore." So writing was terribly valuable to them. They used it first for keeping accounts. Now in Africa, where people can remember genealogies for hundreds of years, they could run large kingdoms without writing.

BALDWIN: I don't know.

MEAD: Why, they did, you know. They ran the largest kingdoms we know about run without writing, because they had this practiced listening rather than looking.

BALDWIN: That is something you still see on the streets of Harlem. One of the hustlers that Malcolm X describes in his autobiography is a numbers runner who never, never wrote down a number. He had them all in his head, thousands and thousands and thousands of numbers. He would know which one you had played and which one I played and what the number paid. He was incredible, a kind of walking computer. And that says something about history too, doesn't it?

MEAD: Yes.

BALDWIN: History must, in one way, be a metaphor for the techniques of survival people have used. And something of that must rest with you forever. How you get it I do not know, though: watching your father, watching your mother, what you hear, I suppose.

MEAD: One of the things that fascinated me for years is that if the black American's rhythm was something that had to be handed down from Africa, how come the white children who were taken care of by black nurses did not have it? And this puzzled me. But I know I've got the answer.

BALDWIN: What do you think it is?

MEAD: You watch the way a black mother carries her own child and the way she carries the white child when she is being the nurse. Have you ever been to Gee's Bend?

Well, it's a forgotten plantation. During the Civil War the white people went away and nobody ever came back. It is in Georgia somewhere, I don't exactly know where. The owners never came back, and the people just kept on living there. They kept the plantation and they lived there and it is just—or it was in the nineteen forties—just the way things were at the time of slavery.

BALDWIN: It's incredible!

MEAD: So you could see things vividly. There weren't any white people there at all, none at all. The mothers carried their children with their backsides sticking out over their arm and their hands under their legs. You know, under the calves of the legs.

BALDWIN: That's right, yes.

MEAD: You see?

BALDWIN: That is the way I used to carry my baby brothers and sisters.

MEAD: Yes. Now when they carried a white child they held it tight. *"Don't* you drop that baby!" You see? A white mistress would be scared to death to have her baby sitting out in outer space, balancing on an arm like that.

BALDWIN: Ha, that's funny.

MEAD: So the same woman, exactly the same woman, conveys one thing to her own child and something different to her little charge.

BALDWIN: Isn't that funny. Isn't that funny. Yet that is true.

MEAD: I'm sure it is.

BALDWIN: I know it's the handling of the baby.

MEAD: You see, when you carry a baby that way you give them everything. When you sort of grab them for fear they'll fall, what you convey to the child is a sense of anxiety and rigidity. When you keep your muscles tight for fear you'll drop them, they tighten up.

BALDWIN: It is true that nothing rubbed off on those white children? I mean, it would appear—

MEAD: Well, certainly nothing rubbed off in the ability to dance and the music and the rhythm. Now we go back to Liverpool: the white mothers and the African fathers who weren't there. So again you just lose the heritage. It is conveyed from parents to children right down. And the speech which you find in black preaching, this marvelous oratory, has the same rhythm as somebody telling about a lion hunt in Africa, with the responses from the audience and everything. So that these are the things which were carried down traditionally and that could be lost.

The black middle class loses them to some extent. It takes two generations. It always takes two generations to really lose something, but in two generations you *can* lose it. And, I think, one of the things that is happening in this country today is the identification of some of the freedom of movement and freedom of touch and use of the ear that has been maintained in black life in this country. And one of the reactions against the rigidity and limitations of—

BALDWIN: Of the dominant white culture.

MEAD: And, you know, I'm not any more limited than you are in my use of English. I don't have as good rhythms as you have, but my rhythms go back ten generations to England. The culture in this country that is so limited, is most limited, is that of the second and third generations away from Europe. They have lost what they had and aren't ready to take on anything else. They are scared to death and so busy being American.

BALDWIN: And that has something to do, doesn't it, with the climate of the country in these present days? The enor-

mous insecurity one feels here about everything? That no
one quite knows who or what he is?

MEAD: Yes, because we have this enormous number of people who came here for only economic reasons. And many
of them expected to go back. Certainly the Italians did.

BALDWIN: Well, in some sense they still do. They intend to
go back to die, anyway.

MEAD: If they can.

BALDWIN: If they can.

MEAD: They came over here and they were still oriented to
the land. They came off the land, and the first thing they
wanted was land. If they got farms in Minnesota they
could fit into a countryside like the one they left. If
they bought a suburban house with a terrible mortgage,
they thought they belonged. They have all the land hun-
griness and all the worry of a European peasant. A great
proportion of them are Roman Catholics, so on top of all
their other problems they see what is happening in the
Roman Catholic Church and it looks as if it was collapsing
around them.

BALDWIN: Which must be rather terrifying.

MEAD: It is terrifying.

BALDWIN: And on top of that the blacks.

MEAD: Who look down on them very often, you know. Because after all the blacks are behaving like the sons of the
American Revolution, too. These would be the immigrants. So these new groups of people who worked so
hard to get a foothold are frightened to death for fear
they are going to lose that foothold. So what we have in
this country at present is a very large number of second-
and third-generation Europeans who aren't really sure
they're here.

Fifteen years ago, if I gave a test for people to fill in: "I

am an American, not a——," most people would say "for-
eigner," and a few said "Communist." Now, they say "not
a Russian," "not an Italian," "not an Irishman," "not a
Pole": over twenty different things.

BALDWIN: It is a curious way to find your identity, labeling
yourself by labeling all the things that you're not. Have
people ever had to do that before?

MEAD: Whenever they emigrated or changed class: the but-
ler's son who goes to Cambridge; the angry young man of
England who reads T. S. Eliot.

BALDWIN: But it has never defined the history of a nation
before: I am an American because I am not a Pole, for
example.

MEAD: It did when people went to new countries, empty
countries. So many new nations were the result of being
empty countries. I think Argentinians . . . all the New
World would do this in a way.

Another fascinating thing: I have a class . . . maybe
twenty students who want to become anthropologists.
Now, if you are going to be an anthropologist you have to
know who you are. You have to virtually go through what
is a sort of cultural analysis—not a psychoanalysis but a
cultural analysis—you've got to be very clear about every
aspect of your ancestors and your religious background.
And we discuss what religion they grew up in and all the
rest of it. We go around the class—

BALDWIN: You are saying that to become an anthropologist
you become your first subject?

MEAD: You have to be your first informant. You have to
interview yourself first on any subject before you interview the other person. I interviewed myself before I
started to talk with you. You have to do that and you have
to watch your dreams, too, when you get into a new cul-

ture; see what you are dreaming and what new things old things are turning into.

BALDWIN: I have always wondered about that whole aspect of my life. Under certain pressures you dream different dreams. For a very long time you don't dream at all or you don't think you do. When I moved back to France I began having terrifying dreams, nightmares. I would wake up screaming. For a long while I could not put my finger on what was going on inside me. I think what was happening was . . . a real terror at finding myself once more displaced. No matter how sophisticated I may be on the surface, no matter how sophisticated anyone is on the surface, at bottom you are not sophisticated, and any rupture is a terrifying thing. It's a little like being born. Or like the fear of falling, which I think is much greater than the fear of death.

MEAD: Fear of falling is primary. You don't know about death until you grow up.

BALDWIN: Exactly. Fear of falling, I think, is the first sensation you ever really have. I think that every crisis brings you back to that first terror in you which lives and lives and lives and will live in you until you die. It's that shift when you move from one place to another; the whole new set of symbols and a whole new set of assumptions. Everything you see is really different, even if they look the same. People in France are not Americans no matter how they may resemble them. And you are a stranger all over again in some incredible situation which you don't know how you are going to manage. I think this must be one of the reasons why people have always tended to cling together and even committed great crimes in the name of a tribe, not so much to protect the tribe as to protect themselves.

MEAD: And it is what young people feel today when they get three hundred thousand of them at a music festival. For the first time they feel safe. And in a sense they were safe, because nobody was going to start arresting three hundred thousand people. And so, as they said about Woodstock, the sweet smell of grass was over it and the police were busy looking for criminals, not for grass. And they were protected by being with each other and not feeling like strangers.

BALDWIN: Precisely. Of course, ironically enough, that situation would drive me up the wall because I'm claustrophobic. I can't stand that many people.

MEAD: Even outdoors?

BALDWIN: Yes. I can't bear being touched and pushed.

MEAD: Have you ever been to India?

BALDWIN: No, I haven't.

MEAD: Don't go. Go to Hong Kong; go where there are Chinese. You can have a million Chinese and they don't touch each other. You put them in any kind of space, and there'll still be a little distance.

BALDWIN: That is why I like the Japanese.

MEAD: And, of course, the Japanese. But in India they're just packed together. You go into a temple and you feel pressed into the crowd.

BALDWIN: I couldn't bear subways for that reason. Years and years ago, when I didn't have a dime, I would walk or take taxis I couldn't afford because of the great pressure of human beings all around you.

MEAD: I used to appeal to subway guards because I was very small. When I was in college I weighed about one hundred pounds, and I would appeal to them as something you could just put in that hole, so they'd push me in.

BALDWIN: That's cute, and rather terrifying.

MEAD: But to get back to my students. . . . They have to
learn these things. They have to learn who they are. So I
ask them to start off with saying who they are. They'll say,
"My maternal grandfather came from Poland." He came
from Ireland or Naples, from somewhere else. I'd say that
the black responses today are quite expectable. They will
discuss racial identity very openly. They identify themselves as black in the very first sentence. They write about
themselves.

BALDWIN: This is all very new. When I was little, we were
ashamed of being black. If someone called you black, he
was insulting you.

MEAD: They are rather expectable in what they say: one
grandparent born in slavery and they lived here and they
lived there and so forth.

But Puerto Ricans say they came from Puerto Rico.
There's nothing back of it, nothing at all. Nothing goes
back to Spain. Nothing goes back to Africa. They came
from Puerto Rico. Haitian peasants believe they origi-
nated in Haiti. The words they use that are African words
are words are words for a mythological country of origin.
It's not seen as a real country of origin.

But you see on an island it is very easy and you don't
get the pressures you get on the continent. Of course,
literate Haitians are some of the most literate people in
the world. But the peasant picture of Africa is only a
mythological homeland. Otherwise, they live in Haiti.

BALDWIN: That's a funny place to be, isn't it? I am trying to
imagine it.

MEAD: Very hard for you to imagine, isn't it?

BALDWIN: It's almost impossible to imagine. Strange though
we are, the line back is very clear and nothing.

MEAD: Very clear. You may not know the individual line, you can't tell whether your ancestors came from Ghana or just where, but the fact that some of your ancestors came from Africa is known.

In New Guinea, I worked for a people there who had very good memories, but they had no sense of genealogy at all. They would go back about six generations. Grandfather's grandfather was as far as they could go, and most people didn't do that. And then when they got the Christian Bible they were delighted. They felt that now they discovered how everything started. They had never known. They said it was very nice to know how things began.

BALDWIN: They had no—?

MEAD: No origin stories at all. None. And they had no future. You see, when a male died he became the guardian ghost of his house. The minute after he died he got very important. They put his skull in the rafters and he bossed the whole household. He made people sick if they didn't do what he wanted. He listened to the wives gossiping and punished them for gossiping. As a ghost he ran things until somebody else died because he hadn't looked after him well enough. Then out his skull went into the sea and the skull of another person came in.

The ex-guardian ghosts became low-level ghosts. People still knew their names and they were around somewhere, but they didn't have any place to house them anymore. Then they became sea slugs and that was the end of that.

BALDWIN: Sea slugs?

MEAD: Little sea slugs. So there was no future and no past.

BALDWIN: Literally a sea slug?

MEAD: Literally a sea slug. But nobody treated sea slugs

with any respect. It was just saying that they were in limbo: they don't matter; they are nothing.

Now, to those people we suddenly brought modern civilization. They thought that every one of us could name our particular ancestors back to Adam. And they felt very inferior because they didn't have the link from grandfather's grandfather to Adam. They were so relieved when I told them we couldn't get back to Adam either. In fact, most of us couldn't get back more than three or four generations, and then we latched onto kings and queens and people like that.

BALDWIN: Ha, what a revelation that is, though!

MEAD: So many things one wouldn't have thought of. Another fascinating thing, for example, was that I didn't realize that they didn't understand printing. They had seen books, and when I went back in 1953 they had set up a school of their own. The man who was running it only had two years of school, but he was running a school. They wanted to have a modern school. And then I got five copies sent to me of a paperback edition of the book that I had written about them twenty-five years before. Five copies came out at once, and their eyes nearly popped out of their heads. Five! Now, they had seen typewriters. They understood typewriting perfectly well. I had a typewriter in 1928, and during the war they had only one million United States servicemen there. But they had never seen two copies of the same book at once. They thought they were typewritten and each book was made separately. The idea that we had something that would make all those books at once just delighted them. They stayed up for hours discussing what a good invention that was.

BALDWIN: As we once did, too, I suppose.

MEAD: Yes, once upon a time.

BALDWIN: It must be very healthy. It must be very humbling to be confronted with—the word is not really ignorance, is it?

MEAD: No. We only talk about ignorance of something that is known. We don't have a word for the impossibility of knowing something yet.

BALDWIN: Exactly. There isn't a word for that, is there? No word that I know. And yet that is where everybody begins.

MEAD: And everybody is at some stage of it. So we can't take somebody at fifty and criticize them for not really knowing what the bomb is. And it isn't ignorance. We need a word for it. Really.

BALDWIN: Why isn't there any word?

MEAD: Because we have always spoken from the point of view of the people who know, and from the point of view of the people who know, the other people are ignorant because they don't know.

BALDWIN: That says a lot about us, doesn't it?

MEAD: Well, it says a lot about the history of civilization and about people who know. After all, the people who know are the ones that write the books. Before they wrote the books they set up the genealogies. And they have always censored the truth, if you want to call it the truth rather than the actuality.

BALDWIN: Yes, that's exactly the thing black kids are reacting against now: the knowledge that white people write history and in a sense wrote them out of it. Not in a sense; in fact.

MEAD: But you see, people wrote all the common people of the world out of it, too. My child's great aunt wrote one of the first books that included the common people in history, though it wasn't written about common people. And there was a book that came out in the forties, edited by Lena Ware, with anthropologists in it, and it represented one of the first times that scholars really discussed seriously the history of nonliterate peoples.

BALDWIN: There is a vast amount of history to be written. In Istanbul I realized that the whole history of the Ottoman Empire did not include the people. It was not for them. And nothing has been written as far as I know, unless it was very, very recently, about the fate of the average person, the average Turk, who was a subject of that empire. And now it is very crucially 1970. Suddenly you have a whole horde of students and semi-intellectuals whose identities have no real basis.

MEAD: And also the Turks went through that terrific shift in the language, a shift which made their written past unavailable.

BALDWIN: Which made their past completely inaccessible, so that a man of fifty in Turkey now is speaking a different language than a boy of twenty. They cannot really communicate with each other which, I think, has very serious repercussions and very sinister implications.

MEAD: Right through the society.

BALDWIN: All the way through it. It means, for one thing, that the intellectuals have become by definition, more and more useless to their country. They really have no contact with the country or the country with them. On the other hand, they are not Western—or modern—yet. It is a very curious bag to be in.

And in some sense it is true for everybody, that they contain their history, or the lack of it, and that you are always the receptacle of what has gone before you, whether or not you know it and whether or not you can reach it. Isn't that true?

MEAD: It's true. But you can break it. You really can break it. Years ago, if we had a group of Italians in a city, we'd try to put Italian in as a course at the university but they wouldn't take Italian. Their parents spoke a dialect and were nonliterate, and taking Italian made them feel inferior whereas taking French made them feel superior. So you can break the connection of a people at any point by picking them up bodily and taking them somewhere else and separating them all from their former relatives and countrymen.

Now, I want to tell you about the other funny people in my class. I get a student who says, "Well, I don't know very much about my ancestors. I think they were sort of English, or Scotch or Welsh, or maybe some Dutch. I don't really know much about them." They are almost always Junior League-D.A.R. people. They actually know in every case. They probably can trace eight lines of ancestry, and they have been taught to be ashamed of it. So, they muddle around and look down.

"We're sort of monglers," I was taught to say as a child. Monglers is a Pennsylvania dialect word for a dog of mixed background. My mother would say that we were members of the intellectual proletariat. In the next breath she would say what she thought of the people in Pennsylvania that hadn't come over here until sixteen eighty!

There was one girl in one of my classes who had the most extraordinary mixed ancestry: she was partly Cuban, partly Mexican, but she had one West Virginia old American ancestor. And she had an absolute tone of voice that she had gotten from this grandmother. So, she said she really didn't know where she came from exactly. She

knew perfectly well about these other ancestors but they
didn't come in. She had the tone of voice of people who
play down their ancestors that they are too proud of.

You see, I think we have to get rid of people being
proud of their ancestors, because after all they didn't do a
thing about it. What right have I to be proud of my grandfather? I can be proud of my child if I didn't ruin her, but
nobody has any right to be proud of his ancestors.

BALDWIN: Yes. I was just wondering about my own, in fact. I
don't know anything about my black ancestors, obviously,
and nothing at all about the white ancestors.

MEAD: You don't know who they were at all?

BALDWIN: No, I just know I have an English name, and God
knows how I got that! But I think you are right. That is a
very, very tricky thing, though, isn't it? Let us say I can
claim Frederick Douglass as one of my ancestors. I am
very proud of him because I think he was a great man and
in some way handed something down: his indignation
was handed down; his clarity was handed down.

MEAD: Well, the fact that you claim him is important. The
fact that you were brought up with the general idea that
he was an ancestor can be important, because that gave
you a style of thinking and pride.

BALDWIN: That is what I mean when I say it is very tricky. I
can see what you mean perfectly well: no one has a right
to be proud because you have nothing to do with it and
yet—

MEAD: And you don't even know whether you have any particular genes or not.

BALDWIN: No, you don't even know that. You have no idea
what is handed down or how. It does not make a difference now, anyway. And yet one's ancestors have given
one something, just the same. It is something difficult to

get at. You know it when you are in trouble, in real trouble. It's true for me and I am sure it must be true for everybody else, one way or another. It is not exactly that you hear a voice. It's just that you pull yourself together to confront whatever it is according to some principle which does not exactly exist in your memory but which has been given.

MEAD: In the name of your ancestors.

BALDWIN: In the name of your ancestors; let us put it that way. I have heard myself walking around the house singing a song I had forgotten, or didn't even know I knew, because I had to get through something and I had to find the only weapons I had. You reach out behind you and pick up whatever there is to confront this moment and to get past it. There is something very mysterious about it. Mystery is the only way I can define it. It is not mystical, but it seems to me that your ancestors give you, if you trust them, something to get through the world.

MEAD: Which means in effect that your parents gave you trustworthy ancestors to be proud of. Suppose you had been adopted as a child and never heard about them? Then you'd have no access to them, though they could be just as real biologically.

BALDWIN: Yes, but that kind of adoption would mean the breaking of the connection, wouldn't it? What about someone who's a bastard?

MEAD: Bastards specialize in knowing who their fathers are. In many parts of the world they know better than their legitimate cousins. They pay more attention to it.

BALDWIN: Because it is much more important.

MEAD: Yes, well, this is the father that hasn't owned you. So this can become a terribly important thing. But I think that one of the things we have got to sort out in America is the recognition of whatever we know about our ancestors. That is the reason I was talking about the woman legislator, Mrs. Hamilton, recognizing her grandfather. This is important, and people should recognize their mixed ancestry if they have mixed ancestry. How much access they have through a kind of physical identification is different. But they also have to realize that all people who came to this country can be treated as our ancestors.

BALDWIN: In fact, have to be.

MEAD: We can take Thomas Jefferson and we can take Crispus Attucks and we can take—

BALDWIN: The American Indian.

MEAD: And the American Indian. The one thing you really ought to be allowed to do is to choose your ancestors.

BALDWIN: Because finally, in a sense you do, don't you?

MEAD: Sure. You pick the people that you care about. How they wrote, in your case. American scientists usually put up in their offices their genealogy, their scientific genealogy. And orthodox American psychoanalysts always have a picture of Freud. There are virtually as many views of Freud as there are of Christ, and which one they pick is very interesting—the young Freud, the old Freud and so forth—whichever, he's there. He's their ancestor. Now, we have a term for this in anthropology: mythical ancestors. And scientists—say you're a chemist; you line up the whole line that you go back to: your teacher and his teacher and his teacher. They are spiritual and mental ancestors, they're not biological ancestors, but they are terribly important.

BALDWIN: We are talking about the models that the human race chooses to work from, in effect. It is difficult to imagine anyone choosing Hitler as an ancestor, for example.

MEAD: There are people who would.

BALDWIN: Who do, yes.

MEAD: Quite a few of them.

BALDWIN: It gets to be rather frightening when you think about it, because it runs very close to the terms in which one elects to live and the reasons for that election. It reveals that depth of whatever dreams you have, and everyone lives by his dreams, really.

MEAD: You know, de Gaulle created a great deal of confusion by remarking to some unimaginative American in the beginning of the Free French Movement: "I'm not Joan of Arc." The American couldn't understand why he said it. What was he talking about? he wondered. And, of course, in a sense he was Joan of Arc.

BALDWIN: Of course he was!

MEAD: He was just trying to separate himself a little from Joan of Arc.

BALDWIN: Churchill said, "I know he thinks he is Joan of Arc, but you won't let me burn him."

MEAD: So that one of the problems in this country is knowing who you are biologically. Some people have this biological access to Indians and Africans and Europeans, so they have access to three traditions. Some have only two and some have only one. There are very, very few black people, of course, who don't have some white ancestors. There are a few.

BALDWIN: There are a few but very few.

MEAD: They are very isolated, usually. A few have moved around. There are a few people in upper New York State, for example, who dropped off from the underground railroad, enough of them to marry each other and form a little community. But it is very rare. A lot of studies have been made, and we know it is exceedingly rare.

BALDWIN: I suppose it is like that in Puerto Rico, too. That is

a curious situation, the whole Puerto Rican thing. I do not
know what they are going to do with it. When the boy you
mentioned said, "I'm from Puerto Rico," I know what he
meant. When they got here they looked like me and they
had come off an island where everybody looks more or
less like me and where everybody speaks Spanish. Then
suddenly they find themselves in America next to the
American Negro, whose existence they had never really
heard of. And he didn't speak Spanish—that's one shock.
On the other hand, the American Negro next to the
Puerto Rican thought the Puerto Rican was speaking
Spanish in order not to be identified with him. And when
the boy said, "I'm from Puerto Rico," the American Negro thought, He means he is better than I am. Now, the
boy didn't mean that, at least not in the beginning.

MEAD: He did later.

BALDWIN: He did later, yes. But in the beginning he only
meant that he was from Puerto Rico and, I suppose, he
had to hold on to that because that was the only thing he
had. And, suddenly, here is this incredible melting pot, or
whatever it is—

MEAD: Well, it isn't a melting pot, is it?

BALDWIN: No, it isn't. Nobody ever got melted. People
aren't meant to be melted.

MEAD: That old image from World War I is a bad image: to
melt everyone down.

BALDWIN: Because people don't want to be melted down.
They resist it with all their strength.

MEAD: Of course! Who wants to be melted down?

BALDWIN: Melted down into what? It's a very unfortunate
image.

MEAD: Sometimes there are images. . . . They made a
cover for a magazine once in Hawaii, where you have

people from everywhere in the world. Around the edges they put faces that were unmistakably Asian, African, Polynesian, Caucasian. Then as you moved toward the center the faces became less and less definite, until you reached the center, where you had a face that you couldn't place. It was beautiful. And of course you see this all the time in Hawaii.

BALDWIN: That's very beautiful.

MEAD: But you couldn't have that face in the center representing the human race if you did not have all the extremes which contributed to it.

BALDWIN: But where this takes us, I do not know. I really do not know. I can't any longer find the point of departure. Part of it is, of course, the great dispersal of the Africans. But then everyone has been dispersed all over the world for one reason or another. And how out of this one arrives at any kind of sense of human unity, for lack of a better phrase, is a very grave question and obviously would take many, many generations to answer. It will take generations, for example, just to redraw the map of Africa, which is now an absolute shambles.

MEAD: We do that every week and come to despair. That is one of the things that has really retired a large number of the older generation. They just can't keep up with the map of Africa.

BALDWIN: All of Africa is sort of invented. Of course it has had a terrible effect on the people who live on that continent. Insofar as the Africans have begun to become self-conscious in the twentieth-century sense, they have begun to become aware that Gambia, for example, once was a part of another country which has disappeared.

MEAD: And following the colonial boundaries has been frightful.

BALDWIN: That is what I mean, really.

MEAD: And the same thing is true of the countries in Indochina. These are all invented countries, invented at a conference table in Europe at which the people who lived there had nothing to do.

BALDWIN: A conference table in Europe where the indigenous people were simply at the mercy of various madmen, madmen plotting in Europe. You know, the spheres of influence, et cetera.

MEAD: I don't think they are mad. You say that so often, and I just don't think they're mad. If a system is archaic and you don't yet know it is archaic, you sound mad.

BALDWIN: Well, yes, that is probably exactly what I mean. But in some sense you are. The power in England is, I think.

MEAD: I'll tell you who else is mad: an illiterate American. They end up in mental institutions. They become paranoid from the simple fact of not reading and writing when other people do. On the other hand, Haitians in New York aren't going to go mad, because their illiteracy is not out of tune. I mean, they came from another country and they learned to manage this. But somebody who grew up here and should have learned to read and write and didn't, he spends his life cheating; he goes mad. I mean, in the end such people often have to be hospitalized.

BALDWIN: I watch that happen very often.

MEAD: On a TV show, Peter Ustinov described a terribly ancient general in the Crimean War who just couldn't get it into his head that the French were on the English side, and every time anybody told him the French were coming he said, shoot them, go out and get them. His men had to shout, General, they are on our side! Now, in a sense, he was mad-disoriented.

BALDWIN: It seems to me there is something a little mad about sitting in, let us say, London or Versailles, looking at the map of Africa and drawing lines on it as though there were no people there.

MEAD: Well, very recently I had a conference with some of the people who were working under a Netherlands grant to the United Nations on behalf of what is now Irian (West New Guinea). It was before the plebiscite, and some studies that were going to be made in connection with the World Bank and things like this. And they said, "Well, we don't think we'll have much difficulty when we survey the minerals and look at the timber and other resources. We think the only thing there that may be some trouble are the people."

BALDWIN: It's not so long ago that the Filipinos were described in the American press as the one argument against our taking over a very valuable piece of real estate. But it was hoped that the Filipinos would have the grace to die out.

MEAD: There was one story, ages and ages ago, about Filipinos having tails. And it went on and on and on. I think it was in the ninth century that the Chinese described the Japanese as little yellow devils, and the Japanese never forgave them. This perpetuation of derogatory epithets drives people crazy in the world. This is one of the things that we will have to somehow try to stop. We worked very hard on this in the 1940s. We said the *noun* is American. We won't say American Negro, we will say Negro Americans, Italian Americans, Japanese Americans. The noun is American. We worked hard at this, and it was supposed to be good. And then, after the war, Australia brought in enormous numbers of immigrants from Europe. They were trying the same sort of thing. They called them new

Australians, very carefully, and the press was instructed to
say new Australians. Pretty soon you began reading in the
press: "Three robberies last night by new Australians."
You were not allowed to say whether they were Dutch or
Hungarian, but—

BALDWIN: But the term became a term of opprobrium by
the weight of the will of the people, really.

MEAD: And this attempt to change the scene by changing
words, which we try so much in the United States—

BALDWIN: It doesn't work, does it?

MEAD: You can say some things with it. Several of my black
colleagues who are over fifty say *"black, Negro, Afro-
American"* in every sentence, because they don't know
what they are going to get attacked for. What I try to do is
if I am saying "In 1941 we said——" I say *Negro*, I do not
say *black*. But I try to get *black* into the next sentence, so
that it is perfectly clear that I know what I should say
now. I know what I said then, but if I go back to 1942 and
put *black American* in my own mouth when I would have
been shot if I said *black American* then, it's nonsense.
You see?

BALDWIN: Yes, anyone would have been shot.

MEAD: It's nonsense. And so we all move around now, in
this funny world. You have been in different English-
speaking countries. You understand what they say, but
you don't know what to ask for in the store. So you say
please turn off the *spigot, faucet, tap*. And if they say to
you *tap* or *spigot* or *faucet*, you know what it is. So what's
happening is making people more tongue-tied, because
they are not quite sure what they should say to this group
or that group when things change so rapidly. Have you
learned to say *Chicano?*

BALDWIN: No, not really. It is absolutely new for me. I don't even know where it came from and I don't even quite know what it means!

MEAD: It means Mexican, in the United States; Mexican on the Pacific Coast, at present.

BALDWIN: That's right, that's where I picked up the expression. I didn't know how to use it. I didn't know whom to ask. Do you know what I mean? It really is kind of frightening, because you don't want to use it. I hate people—hippies, for example—who pick up various black phrases and use them to death and don't know what they are talking about. I never want to be caught in that bag myself. So I have become rather tongue-tied, too. I don't know what to say. I don't know what that means.

MEAD: And, of course, in dealing with Africa, you have this every minute. For example, is it all right to say *French-speaking* and *English-speaking* at present?

BALDWIN: I don't know what to say. I don't know what to say at all. Portuguese Africans, for example. . . . I don't know. What I do is sort of swim around the conversation looking for a straw, waiting for some revelatory phrase which will help me.

MEAD: In World War II everybody stopped telling ethnic jokes in the United States. They were particularly afraid—

BALDWIN: Well, not everybody.

MEAD: Well, we changed them all to moron jokes. All the Irish jokes, the Negro jokes: all the jokes were about morons. If you were jammed in a car with other people, standing all the way from Washington to New York, and you couldn't tell who was behind you and you didn't want to get a swift kick in the ankle, you told moron jokes. You see, nobody was going to say "I'm a moron, don't talk about me." So all the stories were told about morons.

BALDWIN: But they were the same stories.

MEAD: The same stories, exactly; they were just transmuted. And I think that has got some kind of lesson in it, too.

BALDWIN: It does, yes. What it comes to, in a way—doesn't it?—is that what we call racism would seem to be endemic to human nature. When one is complaining about racism and fighting it, what you are really talking about is power. For example, I don't really object to whatever the governor of Alabama may think he thinks about me. I really don't care what he thinks about anything. But I do object to his being the governor of Alabama. That's where it tends to be crucial.

MEAD: I think we'd still better emphasize the self-image point. It shifts more than we give it credit for. I found a health questionnaire—this is in the 1940s—and one of the questions was: "Why should you comb your hair?" This was for the second and third grades. The right answer is: "To keep your hair out of your eyes." And little black boys whose hair couldn't have gotten into their eyes, and who knew it, all gave the right answers and got one hundred percent on it.

BALDWIN: Yes, and were started on the road to madness.

MEAD: Yes. So I watched it, I kept it. I thought, Some day I'll get the opposite.

Right across the river from Mrs. Eleanor Roosevelt's home was the Wiltwyck School for Boys, which was primarily for black juvenile delinquents, but sometimes they got white ones who had worn out their welcome in white institutions. They would end up at Wiltwyck. A black student who was teaching there told me that Mrs. Roosevelt used to invite them for a picnic every year, and in the middle of the night before the picnic he heard a little timid knock on his door. When he opened the door, here was one of the little white boys who wanted some grease to put on his hair like the others.

And you can get that kind of change, you see. I think our sense that things won't change is false. A tremendous number of them will. Now, the fear of someone who is different, especially when he is extremely different, is not going to be so easy to eradicate. You have to have a lot of experience. You have got to really have been loved and touched by people who look very different, if you are not going to be frightened. That is very important both ways. You have to have known enough children of another group when you were a child to realize that some of them are mean and some of them are lovable. Because you build up stereotypes when you know only one or two. That is one reason it is so important for people to live close together and go to school together.

BALDWIN: When I was brought up in Harlem, Harlem was very different than it became later. There were still white people there. There were some Jews left and some Italians and a few Finns down the block. They were all rather odd, but in a way I suppose that has a lot to do with me. I fought every campaign in the Italian-Ethiopian War with the son of the Italian grocer who lived next door. He beat me up regularly—he was much bigger than I till— we got weary of it and we got to be friends. It gave me an insight into Italians which was very useful to me much, much later, when I found myself in Greenwich Village surrounded by Italians, all of whom looked very hostile. And since I knew something about them, I wasn't afraid of them. And that made the difference. We had fights indeed, but they didn't last long because I could call names, too.

MEAD: You knew which names to call them.

BALDWIN: I knew which names to call them, because I had been doing it all my life. And so I survived the Village, though otherwise I never would have.

MEAD: And, of course, this is what the attempt in this country to build more variegated communities is about.

BALDWIN: You can't build a community that way.

MEAD: Well, you can do some things. To begin with, if you have housing that is of differential cost, you have a much better chance of having a variegated community than if you build a town that is so zoned that people can't live there when they retire, and schoolteachers can't live there, and people who work with their hands can't live there. Then you're dead certain you are not going to have a variegated community.

BALDWIN: When I grew up we lived in what was recognized as a neighborhood. Everybody vaguely knew everybody else. We knew the man who ran the drugstore, the man who ran the butcher shop. We may not have liked all these people, but there they were. Later on, when they started tearing down the slums, as they said, and building these hideous barracks, the neighborhood disappeared. There was no longer any communication between the people. There was no longer any way for them to adjust to each other. They were all trapped in these ghastly high-rise slums and hating it. People wondered why they broke the windows and peed in the halls, but I knew why. They were being corralled into hovels like rabbits; they were not being treated like human beings. The tenement that I grew up in, horrible as it was, was better than what replaced it.

MEAD: You mean humanly better?

BALDWIN: Yes, humanly better, because in some way you

were forced to deal with it. There was something to deal with.

MEAD: I heard recently about a skyscraper that had been built for a university faculty, where the children of the university faculty people did the same destructive things as in many other housing projects. It was a response to the inhumanness of this style.

BALDWIN: To the anonymity of it. The anonymity of it is a tremendous insult. People won't bear it. People will become monstrous before they will bear it.

MEAD: Well, what we hope we will get, when looking ahead, is a world where the things that have to be managed on a large scale—like roads, power lines, oil pipelines and all of those things—will be treated rationally and run on a continental or maybe a planetary basis. Then, in the interstices, we will be able to build humanized communities.

BALDWIN: Well, that is what the black thing in America is about, too. The whole battle about schools is a very important and significant battle, and on at least two levels. That is to say, we're speaking as black people insisting on the right actually to supervise our children's education and be responsible for the schools they go to. It is very important, because one no longer can trust most white Americans to do that. They bring their history with them, and their attitudes with them. On the other hand, the reason why the school battle is such a fiasco, again, involves the nature and the structure of power in these present days. In order for us to administer our own schools, millions of dollars have to be liberated into our black hands, and that, of course, upsets and menaces what we will call the power structure. And that battle is what is really the crucial battle going on now in the world: to get out of the hands of the people who have the

means of production and the money, to get it out of their
hands and into the hands of the people at various local
levels so that they can control their own lives.

MEAD: I know you said fairly often that it doesn't cheer you
up to know the Irish had a hard time. But I do think that
if we look at American cities and look at the fate of the
immigrants into the cities, that it is from that point of
view that you could think of black migrants from the
South as immigrants. They came in, got the worst housing
and couldn't get anywhere until they got political power.
Their struggle for political power is comparable to the
Irish or the Italians. Now, let's return once more to your
nephew. You were not going to have him live the life you
have lived. Are you talking about your nephew, an identified child that you know, or are you using him as a metaphor?

BALDWIN: Well, both. I am talking about a certain little boy
that I know, whose diapers I've changed and whom I love.
He just got his first set of teeth or is getting his first set of
teeth and just learned his first words. So, I mean him
literally. I am also perfectly aware that his life is not really
in my hands except to a limited extent. His life is going to
have to be in his own hands. But I am talking about the
world in which he was born, and the set of assumptions
which that world holds about his life. And, when I say
that I won't allow it to happen twice, I won't allow him to
live the life I've lived. I mean that I am determined,
something in me is determined, to do everything in my
power to break the assumptions which can kill not only
him but your child, too.

I am really talking about the new Jerusalem, to tell the
truth. But I think it demands—especially here and now
because we are here and now—a vast amount of passion

and some courage to attack the forces which menace everybody's life. The life of everybody on this planet is menaced by, to put it too simply, the extraordinary and even willful ignorance of people in high places. If the democratic notion has led us to where we now find ourselves, some kind of radical revision of the democratic notion is needed. I do not for a moment, for example, believe that Richard Nixon is the man best equipped to run this country, the man best equipped to—

MEAD: It isn't really Richard Nixon. It isn't really the man. It's the coffee.

BALDWIN: Something about the concept of the office which, it seems to me, has fallen on evil days. Democracy should not mean the leveling of everyone to the lowest common denominator. It should mean the possibility of everyone being able to raise himself to a certain level of excellence.

MEAD: But you see, at present we really are in a world that is unmanageable by the institutions that we have. And when I say this I do not mean capitalism, because it is just as unmanageable in the Soviet Union as it is here; they manage some things better than we do, and we manage some things better than they do. And both of us are polluting the world fast. They are having the same kind of trouble with Lake Baikal that we are with Lake Erie. The real problem is that we are living in a totally new era where all the rules are different, and nobody knows it. And we're all intercommunicating so that we could all go down together and there wouldn't be anybody left.

One of the things that I used to use in communicating with people about the atom bomb was to say that if somebody were to assure me that a million educated people—people who had access to the whole written version of the past and science—could be saved in an atomic war, un-

traumatized, I'd stop worrying. We could start over with a
million people. It would not make any difference where
they were; whether they were a million Chinese wouldn't
matter. But there wasn't any such possibility. Then people said there would be a few Eskimos left. Nobody
knows whether, starting with the culture of the Eskimos
and with a raped earth, we could ever get to where we are
now. And where we are now we are not awfully pleased
with, but it does give us a chance to get to the next place.

So, we have a world that nobody knows how to run. It's
explosive; it could blow up in every conceivable direction.
And we have the chance—you talk about the new Jerusalem. There wasn't any use talking about feeding the world
in the Middle Ages. You fed a few poor people, and a few
Christian people said, "I can't bear to eat well while other
people are starving," so they went into monasteries and
ate poorly. Well, that kept the idea alive. That is the one
thing it did; it kept the idea of Christian charity alive. But
nobody had the food to feed the people. Now we do. So,
now the world looks so evil. And it does look evil at present. It looks so evil because we are just on the edge of
being able to do the things we never were able to do for
it.

BALDWIN: Yes, that is true. And it wouldn't look so evil, I
suppose, if it weren't that terrible contrast between what
we actually do and what we might be able to do.

MEAD: What we actually are able to do. I remember a conference in Washington during the war, when we were
discussing food around the world, and there were people
there—Americans—who were very critical because England wasn't feeding Bengal. Now, examine the picture of
England, surrounded by submarines, without enough
food for her own people. Feeding a country of the same

size in India was a fantastic notion. Of course England was an advanced industrial country. Poor Bengal. You know, there were lots of Americans who really thought that India was sort of smaller than England. They were very surprised when they got there.

So we had to say it wouldn't do any good to take the rubies from the rich, since that would only feed the people for a week, and occasionally they could get so angry they would go and sack the palace and burn it down. That just gratified their feelings; it didn't feed them. Now we are on the edge of being able to feed them. So the fact that today there are people hungry in the United States is *horrible*.

BALDWIN: Because it is unnecessary.

MEAD: Absolutely unnecessary.

BALDWIN: Feeding the hungry is a real possibility. Freedom is a real possibility.

MEAD: The kind of freedom that you can get free. Because today when we have radio and TV you don't have to learn to read and write to know what is going on.

BALDWIN: So what is in the way?

MEAD: We haven't the institutions. We have not developed the mechanisms for doing this. What we call democracy or representative government is really three centuries old —some of it is much older than that—and a very special kind of thing. It assumes the people stay where they are and can pick a representative. You have known him all your life; if he doesn't do what you want, you can do things to him. Everybody has a vote.

Now look what is happening. Half the people in the United States lose their vote because they move all the time. And today the people that have a vote are, on the whole, the most conservative. They want to stay where they are and keep other people out. Whereas the people who move around and lose their votes want the Federal government to take over everything, so wherever they are they will get a good school. We don't know how to handle this yet. And it isn't only voting, it isn't only power lines or organization of cities. We have to do everything at once and this is terrifying.

BALDWIN: Yes. I wonder how it will come about, because some days I have the feeling that some things get done. The kind of changes we are speaking of now, which are very massive and radical changes, come about out of necessity. For example, it occurred to me one day, speaking to some black Englishmen and walking through the streets of London—and I like London and even rather like the English—but it occurred to me that perhaps London will have to disappear before the Africans cease referring to it. If you see what I mean?

MEAD: I understand it. You knock things down but have the memory of them around for two thousand years.

BALDWIN: I don't really mean literally the disappearance of London. And I'm not at all anxious to denigrate the English. That isn't what I really mean either. But the standards which England has represented for so long are now a very crippling set of standards, even for the English.

MEAD: Oh, for everybody.

BALDWIN: For everybody. And in some way they have to disappear. Now, they can disappear in several ways. They can disappear by a kind of concerted effort on the part of the English themselves, or, which is more likely in my judgment, the standards will be taken away from them as being no longer operable. This always involves some degree of social chaos. And I have the feeling that that is what is going to happen in the United States almost certainly. In fact, we are now involved in a dangerous degree of social chaos which shows no signs of getting any better.

MEAD: The thing that worries me, in the United States, is the possibilities of technological chaos. We are so dependent on power. This city could be starved and destroyed so easily, not by revolution in the ordinary sense of the word at all but simply by breakdown.

BALDWIN: Yes, by throwing a few buttons.

MEAD: And how are we going to—at a period when there are so many people who have failed to be fitted into the social system in any way, so they are going around shooting twenty people or throwing bombs at random—how are we going to protect this system which is so vulnerable?

BALDWIN: I don't think, in this case, that it can be protected.

MEAD: It can be protected or we won't be here.

BALDWIN: But how? How? I don't see how one can protect this—

MEAD: Well, just consider for the moment. When you were a little boy, did you ever call the Fire Department?

BALDWIN: Yes.

MEAD: When there wasn't a fire?

BALDWIN: No.

MEAD: But wouldn't it have been fun to call the Fire Department? Can you remember when you were small enough so that having the Fire Department roar down the street—

BALDWIN: Yes, I remember. It was a marvelous thing.

MEAD: And yet most little boys don't either set a fire or—

BALDWIN: Call the Fire Department.

MEAD: —or call the Fire Department. This is really the miracle of the modern world.

BALDWIN: Yes. Why didn't one?

MEAD: I mean this is the thing that I think we have to get at. You know, the fact is that when we have had fires and riots in the ghetto they destroyed their own. Well, not exactly their own. If you put up a sign that said Soul Brother, maybe your shop didn't get burned down. Or if it did, it was because of a fire next door that they couldn't stop. But they limited violence. Now you can say, of course, that this was fear. The reprisal would have been much worse. But I don't think people were thinking about reprisals.

BALDWIN: At that point you are not thinking about—

MEAD: There was a self-limiting factor somewhere. It's demonstrated by the number of these revolutionary kids who make bombs and blow themselves up instead of the thing they said they were going to bomb. There still is in most people who are mad—I mean really mad, though, not the kind of mad you keep calling people but really angry—a lack of destructiveness, a tremendous lack of destructiveness.

BALDWIN: Yes, I would accept that. I don't think that people really want to destroy. But I do think that people can find themselves in a situation so intolerable that destruction appears to be and may indeed be the only answer.

MEAD: That is true. But what they do is destroy their own.

BALDWIN: In the case of the ghetto, I think that that should be slightly clarified. If, for example, oil were discovered under the tenement I used to live in years ago, it is not the people in Harlem who would get rich on the oil. They don't own anything in the ghetto. They don't own the land. This is still the most tremendous question. To be in the ghetto is to be a kind of prisoner, more or less official, of the state. And if nothing belongs to you, there is no reason not to burn it down, especially if it is oppressive.

MEAD: That's right. You burn down the worst things; the most oppressive shops, the worst tenements and so forth.

BALDWIN: It seems to me that people would not be human if they didn't do that either.

MEAD: No, but they are burning down within their own domain. I mean, it is not their domain from one point of view, the point of view that you're stating, but as human beings it is their domain, even though they are in economic slavery.

BALDWIN: That is quite true, and so far it has been, as you put it, the limiting factor. But I think the day is coming when they will cross the ghetto lines. I think the day is almost inevitable.

The reason the police are so hated in the ghetto is not merely because they happen to be, for the most part, rather unattractive human beings, but because you don't have to be more than fifteen years old at the very most to realize that the cop is not there to protect you but to protect Mr. Charlie's property. And that makes his presence absolutely intolerable.

MEAD: Well, how do you explain this? Or maybe you have not heard about it. There was an episode about a month ago in Chicago—after they had started some new program in which the cops were going to communicate with the people—where a cop was killed by a sniper. Now this is pretty dangerous. And the next week, of their own free will, the cops went back into that project where there could have been a sniper on any roof. Now how do you explain it at all?

BALDWIN: I don't know if it has to be explained. I think that in Chicago, and Chicago is a very good example, some of the policemen and some of the people in authority have begun to realize the gravity—you know, the really extreme gravity—of the situation. The South Side of Chicago is really a pretty appalling place. Some policemen must have begun to realize that you simply cannot go around cowing the natives; that the natives have a real grievance and, furthermore, there are many millions of them.

MEAD: But it is a long way from realizing this, and approving the steps to do things, to going out there and risking your own skin when you don't have to. You know, Martin Luther King went places where he knew he might be killed. The small children in school integration proceedings in the South knew what might happen to them; they went. Now when you are getting this on both sides, and especially from a rather unlikely spot on the police force as we have known it, I find this a little hard to explain. You can't explain it. We have got to postulate a moral force at work on both sides to explain that courage.

BALDWIN: I accept that. A great deal of what I say just leaves me open, I suppose, to a vast amount of misunderstanding. A great deal of what I say is based on an assumption which I hold and don't always state. You know my fury about people is based precisely on the fact that I consider them to be responsible, moral creatures who so often do not act that way. But I am not surprised when they do. I am not that wretched a pessimist, and I wouldn't sound the way I sound if I did not expect what I expect from human beings, if I didn't have some ultimate faith and love, faith in them and love for them. You see, I am a human being too, and I have no right to stand in judgment of the world as though I am not a part of it. What I am demanding of other people is what I am demanding of myself. Do you see what I mean?

MEAD: Yes. But I think you have to expand it to realize that there are things happening on both sides of the lines that are being drawn.

BALDWIN: Oh, I know that. I have watched it. I have lived too long and too hard a life and been saved by too many improbable people not to realize that.

MEAD: But it is a very serious question at present. Whether people say that there has been so much more polarization—

BALDWIN: I am not entirely misled by the way things seem to be.

MEAD: They're so played up, you know.

BALDWIN: Yes, I know that. I always think, too, that every force creates a counterforce. And the polarization one is speaking of has also driven some people much closer together and has had the advantage, in any case, of making things much clearer. It is much, much harder to fool yourself about the situation in this country now than it was even five years ago. If you have any sense at all, any eyes at all, you can see where we are and how grave the danger is.

MEAD: And we are still waiting—each town is waiting for its own riot.

BALDWIN: Its own holocaust.

MEAD: We are doing exactly what happened in World War II in England. Those cities that didn't get bombed were lax in all their precautions. Little cracks of light were showing through the blackout and fire watchers weren't working and people went around saying, "What this city needs is a good bomb." Well, that is what we have been waiting for. One of the reasons, I think, that we have had as much violence as we have had is that the people who should have been on the other side, or that one would expect to be on the other side, who wanted something to

happen and did not have any way of making anything
happen, unconsciously fed the violence so that the violence would produce some kind of change. This certainly
has happened on the college campuses.

BALDWIN: The effect of the violence paralyzes a great many
American people, who simply can't face what it means.

MEAD: I think it is very bad only to respond to violence and
not respond long before there is violence.

BALDWIN: But, alas, most white people until this hour, for a
complex of reasons which there may be no purpose in
going into, partly willfully and partly out of genuine ignorance and a lack of imagination, really do not know why
black people are in the street. And God knows, the mass
media do not help to clarify this at all.

Every time you see a riot, you see all of these people
stealing TV sets and looking like savages, according to the
silent majority's optic. If you do not know why they are in
the streets—especially with various ivy league colleges
and Arrow-collar-ad men, and all the symbols and tokens
of progress—there is a danger of another polarization, at
least on the surface. Because then the world, the white
American and the world, looks at, let us say Harry Belafonte, to use arbitrarily a famous public figure, and those
people rioting on the South Side, and they conclude, as
they are meant to conclude, really, that if those people on
the South Side washed themselves and straightened up
they could all be Harry Belafonte. There is nothing wrong
with the system, so the American thinks; there is something wrong with the people. This is the greatest illusion,
and the most dangerous delusion of all, because it exacer-
bates the rage of the people trapped in the ghettos. They
know why they are there, even if America doesn't.

MEAD: A few years ago there were so many people saying

that there was not going to be any trouble in Detroit. Why? Because Negroes had done better in Detroit than any other city. There were a lot of rich black people. Now, Detroit had one of the worst riots just because there were black people who owned yachts and Cadillacs and all that.

BALDWIN: I said that the black people who hate white people most are not the people on the level of the porter but what we would have to call the black middle class. They are the closest to American aspirations and by far the most frustrated.

MEAD: But also, as long as the poor could believe that if some of the barriers were removed they could have a yacht, which was in a sense a symbol of education and—

BALDWIN: Acceptance.

MEAD: The black parents who picked cotton to send ten children to college from the 1930s on thought those children could just get an education and there would be a little relaxation and they could get there. Now, the young people in this country, the poor, black or white, know that they can never get there. And yet they see it every day in front of them.

BALDWIN: Which, in a way, is very healthy. I have never accepted the notion that you keep a Cadillac or a yacht or anything at all, except perhaps for convenience. I have always had a quarrel with this country not only about race but about the standards by which it appears to live. People are drowning in things. They don't even know what they want them for. They are actually useless. You can't sleep with a yacht. You can't make love to a Cadillac, though everyone appears to be trying to. And the kids hate them, as is now beginning to be evident. The kids can't live with them at all. I think the great emotional or psychological or effective lack of love and touching is the key to the American or even the Western disease.

MEAD: Well, I think probably more here but—

BALDWIN: Well, here it is a most exaggerated form.

MEAD: But most people who came here were terribly poor and wanted things.

BALDWIN: To prove they existed.

MEAD: To prove they could get them at all. They had been eating the black bread of poverty, so they came over here and they wanted to eat the white bread that was eaten in the castle. So instead of eating good, nourishing, whole wheat bread—

BALDWIN: They started eating white bread. Yes, indeed, look at the results.

MEAD: They began eating too much sugar too; that's what the people in the castle had. So that what we have here, and I think this has to be remembered, is not an old American style. Old Americans were frugal. The style in this country . . . I still—you know, I was brought up to untie each package carefully, untie the knots in the string and roll it up and put it away to use again.

BALDWIN: Yes, I still do that too. And I hate myself for it.

MEAD: Still, there were all these people who thought they were coming to a land where the streets were paved with gold, and *that* is the reason they came. Now, if you go somewhere and suffer quite a lot trying to get there, being poor and digging roads, living in slums when you first come, and you only came because the streets were paved with gold—

BALDWIN: That describes a great deal of the black man's ironical amusement when he watches white people. You know, he did not have that illusion. He didn't want to come.

MEAD: He didn't come with that illusion at all. Now, most of the people who came to this country were poor. We had very, very, very few people who came to this country who had anything.

BALDWIN: People who were making it in England obviously didn't get on the Mayflower. Everybody knows that.

MEAD: They were youngest sons who were disinherited.

BALDWIN: Various convicts. Fallen and loose ladies.

MEAD: They were all the tenth child in the family, tenth or ninth or—

BALDWIN: Or the poor Irish looking for the potato.

MEAD: Because they were starving at home. And the dream of the starving is not—

BALDWIN: The dream of the starving is to be fed.

MEAD: Yes, that's it. And the dream of the people who have nothing is to have things. If you haven't had a chair to sit on and haven't had a spoon to eat with—

BALDWIN: The great revolution that one has . . . that one has dared. . . . The dream of the starving is not only to be fed. This is what you meant when you asked me that question about my great-nephew. One has got to arrive at the point where one realizes that if one man is hungry everyone is hungry. Isn't that true?

MEAD: Yes.

BALDWIN: That is what's really at issue.

MEAD: But that's now. It wasn't any good realizing that before.

BALDWIN: You mean it could not have been realized before.

MEAD: It could not have been realized. Well, we use *realized* in the other sense, you know. What I hope is going to happen in the world is a demand similar to the one in this country, the demand for a simpler form of life. Coming up from the kids of the affluent middle class who say,

"We don't want to live like this. We don't want to over-capitalize the individual home this way. We want to make things much more collective." Then maybe we can invent a style in this country that is viable for other countries. Because otherwise what is happening is that other countries are copying this style, so the few educated and elite can get themselves some Cadillacs and big houses. Then all of the rest of the people are miserable. Also we are bleeding the world of its resources and we can't do that.

So what is the American dream? The American dream of old Commodore Vanderbilt—What did he borrow? Two hundred dollars from his mother and started bringing potatoes over from Staten Island—who ended up building palaces. But they were not palaces of kings. They were palaces of people who had had nothing and wanted things. And then I go back to my Manus people in New Guinea, who said, "When you have plenty, then you can afford to begin to think about human beings. And when you don't have, you don't think about human beings."

BALDWIN: Well that is both true and not true. I don't want to be sentimental about poverty, which is a hideous condition. I once flew from Istanbul to Switzerland. Istanbul is exceedingly poor. But the people will give you anything they have, and there is a kind of human warmth which you do not find on the streets of Lausanne.

MEAD: Where everybody's well off.

BALDWIN: Yes. And you wouldn't dream of asking anybody for the time of day.

MEAD: Well, you can produce a kind of private-property-oriented society where they also have the private property, where they don't have any free energy for anyone else at all.

BALDWIN: And that, it seems to me, is very common.

MEAD: True. But this country hasn't been a country that hadn't any free energy for other people. I think you have to discriminate between the people who came here early for political and religious reasons—the ones whom we still think made the country and whom we still talk about and use as ideals, and who did come here to live their kind of life the way they believed in—and the great many millions of immigrants who came here in the nineteenth century—

BALDWIN: But they—the idealists—were very rare.

MEAD: Simply because they were driven out at home and they would have starved if they stayed there. They were the most enterprising. They refused to stay home and starve. (Neither did the wetbacks in Mexico stay at home and starve; they swam the river and came to this country to work.) Those who came were not the most fortunate in their own country. The eldest son, who was the heir, didn't come. Look at French Canadians. We have one third of the French Americans, North Americans, in the United States, and they are the "unsuccessful." But what did it mean to be unsuccessful? It meant a father didn't pick that son out to inherit the farm. A mother didn't pick that other son out to get an education. So those children, usually the younger ones, had to leave. You can't really think of them as unsuccessful. But they were badly placed in the system. Most of them weren't idealists. They were looking for *things* because they didn't have any.

BALDWIN: I'm afraid that is true. If it wasn't, I think this would be a very different country now.

MEAD: Well, we still think . . . have the sort of notion, as expressed in Felicia Hemans' poem, "Ay, call it holy ground, The soil where first they trod! They have left

unstained what there they found—Freedom to worship
God."

BALDWIN: That is very unfortunate rhetoric.

MEAD: It isn't entirely unfortunate rhetoric. When Kru-
shchev came to this country, somebody thought up a radio program of books we would like to send him so he
could understand the United States. I picked this poem to
show how people in the United States associate religion
with freedom. That's what they associate it with; that's
what they talk about all through middle America: "Right
to go to my church and nobody is going to stop me!" The
Russians associate religion totally with oppression. It is a
very different picture and it got pickled in these early
days when there were so many religious refugees of one
sort or another. So this is part of our image of what is
American, yours and mine, because our ancestors came
here together. We share a notion of a kind of people that
formed the ideals of this country and the ideals against
which we have always been measuring the country and
finding it faulty. But the ideals were here. I mean, Jefferson *did* postulate ideas of democracy that one could follow.

BALDWIN: Yes, but he also owned slaves.

MEAD: Sure he did. But he set down statements on the
basis of which one could fight for the vote for everybody
in this country. The fact that he owned slaves is one thing.
The principles he laid down are something else. You can
call it rhetoric, but I don't believe you really believe these
things are just rhetoric. They made it possible for us to go
further and have better dreams. But you see, we have
now an enormous amount of people in this country who
didn't come here to dream. They didn't have dreams,
except just security for their children. And these are the

people that we call the silent majority and they are terribly frightened.

BALDWIN: Yes, their fear frightens me.

MEAD: They are terribly easy to frighten, and their fear is frightening. Though all fear is frightening, and certainly all groups that are frightened are frightening.

BALDWIN: Because it may be that their fear will precipitate the kind of social chaos which no society can really survive. This fear can result in a kind of convulsion of apathy.

MEAD: I don't think that there is so much apathy. I think there is an enormous lack of knowledge of what to do about anything. There is an enormous sense of frustration, and people feel so strongly in this country that you ought to be able to fix at once anything that goes wrong. Press a button and something happens. Then they try to manage our political system or our economic system in the same way.

You know, you can't buy a tape recorder that works. You buy one that isn't right and you send it back and they send it back and they send it back again, and you spend six months getting it adjusted. Everybody in the country is in a state of frustration about something. I think irritation rather than apathy is much more important here now. Everybody is irritated. Their skin is sort of scratchy. We always talk about the danger of trouble if the temperature goes up too high in summer. But this irritation is itself like a rising temperature. Apathy isn't the word anymore for what is happening. I don't think people are apathetic in New York when they see somebody attacked on the street. I think they just plain don't know what to do. They don't know whether they will get killed themselves. We had a lovely episode on the subway where a gang of kids were going to attack a girl, and a sailor from the back-

woods just went in and stopped them. But the average
New Yorker doesn't know what to do. The average middle-class person has had no contact with violence.

Once in a child psychiatric clinic I watched a scene
through a one-way glass where they were testing a very
dangerous fifteen-year-old boy. Everybody knew he was
pretty dangerous. The psychologist who was testing him
had a whole set of things laid out on the table, including a
hammer, which was ridiculous to have had there. All of us
were sitting on the other side of the screen, and he knew
that there were people on the other side of the screen.

BALDWIN: The boy knew it?

MEAD: The boy knew; they had been honest with him. He
was spending his time playing with the idea of throwing
that hammer through the screen. Everybody in the room
was playing with the idea of throwing that hammer
through the screen. Everybody in the room was frightened except me because I knew I could dodge that hammer. I have lived among people who don't have shields.
They just catch or dodge spears thrown at them. If you
know the time it takes someone to pick up a hammer, you
can dodge. But nobody else in that room knew they could
dodge. They were just paralyzed with the lack of knowledge of what in the world to do.

BALDWIN: And for a long time only black children were being menaced and slaughtered, too.

MEAD: That brings us to Kent State. Now, I would like to
relate to you a discussion in one of my classes and have
you comment on it. After Kent State, one of the black
students said everybody got excited about Kent State;
then they went back to that previous massacre in
Orangeburg where black students were killed. "Nobody
was excited then," he argued, "and now that white kids

are being killed white people are excited." I said, "And
now that black kids are being killed in Jackson you are
excited. Now if it is right for you to be more interested
and care more about the Jackson kids—" They weren't,
any of them, caring about the white kids at Kent State.
The only point they were making was that when the kids
were killed at Orangeburg nobody cared. I said, "You
cared."

BALDWIN: They meant the country, the country didn't care.

MEAD: The black people in the country cared. Then we
have white kids killed and the white people in the country
care. Then we have more black kids killed and the black
people in the country care. Now, I don't think you can
blame people for caring more, or being more vividly
caught, when someone that they identify with, who might
have been their own child, is killed. If black people are
going to care more about Jackson State—and they did, a
lot more—then you're going to have to expect that white
people are going to care more about white kids. Now—

BALDWIN: Yes, but—

MEAD: You see, you identify the country with the whites.
Now—just before you blow up about this—I want to tell
you what happened next. After they had gone at this with
hammer and tongs, I said, "What about the Italians who
are picketing the F.B.I. as being unfair to Italians because
they are persecuting the Mafia?" This was one of the
cases when you grab for a third instance. The Italians
were making an overriding ethnic identification that was
more important to them than whether the Mafia were
racketeers or not. And I don't think we can do that. I
don't think you can speak of "the country" that way, because there were a *lot of people* who were upset about
Kent State and Jackson State. And there were a lot of

people who were upset about Orangeburg. Now, who are the conscience of the country?

BALDWIN: The conscience of the country has only a certain voice.

MEAD: Only a certain voice. But people are only really going to be affected immediately if something touches them that they can imagine and understand. And so when we say it spreads from the inner city to the suburbs, and then people get excited . . . but the reason the people in the suburbs get excited is because they see what is happening to their kids and the people in the inner city see what is happening to their kids. They are there.

BALDWIN: But my point is not so much that the white people got more upset about Kent State, more upset about white kids being killed than about black kids being killed. That, in a way, is sinister enough. What is most sinister to me is that they cared so little. I am not objecting that they cared too much, I am objecting that they didn't care enough.

MEAD: About Kent State.

BALDWIN: About Kent State.

MEAD: They cared enough to do a hell of a lot of lying.

BALDWIN: A lot of lying!

MEAD: Oh, the distortion.

BALDWIN: Well, of course, that is par for the course.

MEAD: There was a terrific distortion of the Kent State thing. When it was being something to care about, no one discussed the fact that the guards who had been on duty there were being battled with for three days, and that the kids that were in the crowd are the ones that had burned the R.O.T.C. building down. That was all scotomacized, distorted; you had as bad a scotomization as ever happens when they are discussing a black-white situation. It was heavily scotomacized. I think this is a serious thing in this country: the inability to look at the whole situation every time anybody is partisan on one side.

BALDWIN: But this comes back to what you described before, this fact that the whole world has become unmanageable and the institutions cannot respond to the needs of the society. The National Guard should have never, for example, been sent in and should never, never, never have had weapons.

MEAD: Of course they shouldn't.

BALDWIN: That is so obvious by hindsight, but it should have been obvious from before the beginning. There has always been, perhaps not *only* in America, but certainly in this country, a kind of—it's a banal thing to say but I think it's true—a strain of violence. Violence has always been a kind of door to the whole legend of the Western, the cowboys-and-Indians nonsense. I have always considered that whole legend a kind of insult to the human race. You know, the glorification of the slaughter of people becoming a door to American folklore. It says a great deal to me about this country and about the way people are unconsciously trained—schooled—to accept violence. Because there are some people who even think it's true, that noble legend, true and therefore justifiable.

MEAD: I think what makes them accept violence and why we have so much trouble trying to get any arms control legislation is because in this country the gun belongs both to the bad man and to the good man. And the only way the good little guy can get even with a big bad guy is with a gun.

BALDWIN: Yes, but I think that is a very sinister way for people to look upon themselves.

MEAD: Well, in a frontier society, if you have some people walking around with guns, the only way that the weaker person can operate is with a gun. This is in our whole folklore. It's the good guy with a gun who finally—

BALDWIN: Who saves the poor little good guy.

MEAD: Saves either himself or other good guys.

BALDWIN: But I observe that there has been very little salvation accomplished by that means. That is still simply a self-perpetuating myth that involves some kind of adolescent self-love on the part of Americans. I always found it very distressing because it has been one of the things which has prevented Americans from ever really growing up, this simplistic notion that life can be lived that way. After all, we do not now live in a frontier society.

MEAD: Well, the simplistic notion is that there are good guys and bad guys. I mean, that everything is as simple as that.

BALDWIN: Yes, exactly. And look at what America calls its foreign policy.

MEAD: But when you come from so many different cultures and you leave all of their nuances behind and you are at sea, as you described so vividly, in a new country, what you are going to understand are the simplest possible markers. How many dollars, how many A's in school, how many neon lights. And in order to make any comparisons at all—and you have got to make some comparisons—you have got to find out who you want your kids to be like and who you don't want them to be like.

BALDWIN: In that case, you are caught in a very unlucky kind of collision, because that way of measuring the world, that way of measuring reality, is not only archaic but really, again, dangerous.

MEAD: It made mass production possible. We are able to simplify processes.

BALDWIN: And mass production has made human life impossible.

MEAD: No, not really. We never could have things for everybody until we got mass production.

BALDWIN: And what are we going to do with it now?

MEAD: Well, something else. You know, just because the Ford car and the idea of Mr. Ford did give enormous freedom to people in this country, it doesn't mean we have to—

BALDWIN: It didn't give them any freedom, it gave them tremendous mobility.

MEAD: Well, Americans think mobility and freedom are very close together. If you take Detroit, now. . . . A study has just been made that compares somebody without a car only a few blocks away from somebody with a car. The one with a car is not twice as mobile, he is over ten times as mobile.

BALDWIN: This I discovered to my horror when I was living in Hollywood.

MEAD: Well, if you don't have a car—

BALDWIN: Human feet have suddenly become obsolete. There's no point in having feet, except to drive the car. I guess I am badly placed in this society, in many ways. But I see what you mean. I know we had to have these things, we had to have them. I know that it was at one point in human history a tremendous advance for the human race. But now mass production, the consumer society, seems to be one of the things that menace us the most, because we have become so dependent upon it.

MEAD: The automobile in its present shape is a monster. But to envisage a society without automobiles, with the number of people that we have, is also very difficult. We will have to make some new inventions.

BALDWIN: Then we have got to find a way to control this
 . . . this monster we have created.

MEAD: That's right. We have to find different kinds of automobiles, set them up differently.

BALDWIN: And keep them out of the cities.

MEAD: And keep them out of the cities. All these things we
have to do. But it is very different to say, This is terrible;
we should go back somewhere.

BALDWIN: I don't want to go back anywhere! That isn't what
I mean at all!

MEAD: All right, if you don't want to go back anywhere you
have to accept Mr. Ford. Mr. Ford's mass production for
the mass of the people is one of the things that got us
here, you see. So, if you don't want to go back—

BALDWIN: Back to what?

MEAD: Exactly. If you want to go forward from here, then
the steps that got us here have to be incorporated into
where we are going next.

BALDWIN: Well, I think that's the only reasonable way to
look at it. The question is how are we going to do it. And
the question in my mind is time.

MEAD: If we were certain we had one hundred years,
even—

BALDWIN: But we don't.

MEAD: I know we don't. But if we were certain we had that
long it would be very easy to do.

BALDWIN: We are not certain. And we are on a shrinking
globe which is full of people who do not assess reality the
way Americans do, who have the advantage over Americans, as Vietnam proves, because the life which this way
of life has imposed on so many people in the world has
become intolerable for the people of the world, and they

have to overthrow it by whatever means come to hand. *And I mean they have to.*

MEAD: The people at the bottom have always had the power of nothing to lose.

BALDWIN: Yes, and they have always overturned the society.

MEAD: Well, they have changed it somewhat. I don't think any society has ever really been overturned.

BALDWIN: But it can be so badly damaged that it is forced to find new principles by which to live. This is what I mean when I—

MEAD: Put some new tyrants in power.

BALDWIN: Well, alas, there is also—

MEAD: Today, I think we need something newer than the old—

BALDWIN: Than new tyrants? Yes. I don't want to see it happen, but I don't know what else can happen, given the situation in which we find ourselves now.

MEAD: We have the choice now, right this minute, of people putting their energies into trying to control the technological system so that it is workable for human beings, or putting their energies into romantic notions of anarchy and revolution.

BALDWIN: Yes, but that would be—

MEAD: It's a real choice.

BALDWIN: Yes, but the second choice is obviously disastrous.

MEAD: It's disastrous, but it is what is happening.

BALDWIN: I know that's what's happening. That is why I am frightened. It is very difficult to ask people to give up the assumptions by which they have always lived, and yet that is the demand the world has got to make now of everybody. Because the assumptions by which we have all lived so far are as inhuman as the Spanish Inquisition—or the Third Reich.

MEAD: Of everybody, including the romantic assumption that revolution will work without a new design.

BALDWIN: I was a revolutionary at fifteen, but I gave that up the same time I left the church. I am another kind of revolutionary now, if I am a revolutionary at all. I might even be described as a conservative in terms of the things that I think are valuable and want to see honored and made viable for people's lives. But I do know that we are surrounded by poverty and rage, and I know how explosive a formula that is.

MEAD: I know.

BALDWIN: That has nothing whatever to do with reason, nothing whatever to do with human charity. It has to do with human need, and human needs have to find some way of expressing themselves, some way of being met.

MEAD: There is a little bit of a contradiction, because you talked before about all of the kindness and generosity among the poor. Now, there is generosity and kindness among the poor when they think nothing can be done about it on the whole. When they think that something can be done about it, then they are using their energy getting mad and—

BALDWIN: Yes, and trying to change things.

MEAD: And trying to change things. And that's what we have now, I think. Whereas when you were growing up most of the people you knew were pretty resigned to the fact that life was going to be hard. If you got educated maybe you'd get out of it. But it was hard. There wasn't the hope, there wasn't the real hope or dream of as much of a change as there is now, was there? For individuals, yes. But for everybody?

BALDWIN: That's a serious question. I have to think back. When I was growing up it was . . . yes, it is true, there was a kind of resignation. The whole style came out of a certain kind of resignation which is gone forever.

MEAD: I think so.

BALDWIN: Even people who got educated realized that they were still in a trap. I knew too many people who had been to college who were shuffling around with garbage cans to be fooled about what education would do. And now it is very different. It is very different because the image that black people have of themselves has changed. It is utterly changed, and it has changed because of objective reasons. It has changed because the world has changed. It has changed because of what we have seen on television: black leaders, black riots, white liars. It has changed because the power of white people to control my mind—black minds—has been broken, and that is a very important shift. It is perfectly true: no one growing up now has before them the vista that I had when I was growing up. Though that, paradoxically, increases the poverty and the rage, doesn't it?

MEAD: Of course it does.

BALDWIN: And therefore the danger.

MEAD: And therefore the danger.

BALDWIN: That's where we are, though.

MEAD: That's where we are and it's where, in a sense, TV has brought us. Because it has brought everybody's way of life to everybody else.

BALDWIN: Into America's living room. God, that living room! We seem simply to be confronted with enormous questions, just as real as these hideous buildings outside your window. There they are, and what should we do with them? Because they are still not fit for human habitation, for the most part.

MEAD: But we are very short of living space. We really at

the moment can not afford to dispense with any of it. One of the greatest crimes against the people of New York City is the fact the landlords have let buildings go so that we have lost something like one hundred thousand dwelling units in the last few years.

BALDWIN: That is the fault of the system. One has been avoiding the word capitalism and one has been avoiding talking about matters on that level. But there is a very serious flaw in the profit system which is implicit in the phrase itself. And, in some way or another, one can even say at this moment, sitting in this room, that the Western economy is doomed. Certainly part of the crisis of the Western economy is due to the fact that in a way every dime I earn, the system which earns it for me—I don't mean the fact that I write books, but the way the system works, the base—is standing on the back of some black miner in South Africa, and he is going to stand up presently. Now, if we don't anticipate that, we will be in terrible trouble. Because he is not going to be bending under this weight ten years from now. And if we don't understand that and let him stand up, the whole thing is going to be a shambles.

MEAD: I agree. But I also think if we don't understand that if the systems, whether they call themselves private power or public planning, don't learn to think ahead further and include all human beings more, they are contributing to the shambles.

BALDWIN: That is, of course, my point. I don't see at this moment how we are going to avoid it. One day South Africa will blow up. It is as certain as death.

August 27th...11 P.M.

MEAD: Now what's been bugging you all day?

BALDWIN: Enormous question. For me, an enormous question. I still don't know how to put it, quite, but it has something to do with time present. This time and *time*. And those are two enormous concepts, aren't they? Or two enormous facts. I don't know if I can ever get it together. I think that for me, watching my children's children discovering, beginning to apprehend that they have been marked by most unfriendly forces. Watching the time, your eyes get heavier or lighter. . . .

There's a kind of fury in me because I've never quite been able to translate my concern for my two-year-old

into my concern for your two-year-old. The basis of what
I'm trying to say is somehow involved in that. I don't
think I am sentimental about human life, though maybe I
am. But I feel very much like William Blake. I really have
some feeling. . . . You know, we were talking about the
dark gods and the white gods, angels and devils, weren't
we? You are an angel; you look like an angel. It is very
bad for the character. I look like the devil, which is also
very bad for the character.

MEAD: Very bad for the character.

BALDWIN: And what has obsessed me, what I cannot get
clear, is how to achieve that wedding, or really how to
legalize that wedding. Because there is a certain wedding
which has already occurred.

MEAD: That's right, the wedding has been there from the
beginning.

BALDWIN: It is already there. We are the human race. Finally there is only one, isn't there?

MEAD: That's right.

BALDWIN: From New Guinea to Harlem.

MEAD: That's right.

BALDWIN: From Harlem to New England.

MEAD: And from Tokyo to London.

BALDWIN: It doesn't make any difference. So how are we
ever going to achieve some kind of language which will
make my experience articulate to you and yours to me?
Because you and I have been involved for all our lives—I
am younger than you but not very much younger—in
some effort of translation. Isn't that true?

MEAD: Yes.

BALDWIN: Some effort to translate what it means to be born
here, what it means to be born there, what it means to be
born at all. What time means. And the fury in me is in-

volved with time now because I have no right—I may be
a philosopher, but I have no right—given the situation of
this time now, and my role in it, my role in the *present*.
. . . On a very serious level, the trap I'm in is that I can't
afford the historical point of view. And yet I know something about time present and time now. Do you know
what I'm trying to say?

MEAD: Yes, I know what you're trying to say. If people don't
include the historical point of view they can act more
definitely.

BALDWIN: But if you must include the historical point of
view, then you're Hamlet on the battlefield, aren't you?

MEAD: Then you don't do anything.

BALDWIN: Yes. The trouble is that I'm really neither black
nor white. Neither are you, by the way.

MEAD: No.

BALDWIN: When you asked me this morning, before we
started taping, "Why don't you test me?" I said, "I don't
have to test you." You're neither black nor white, either.
Because, as Malcolm X put it, white is a state of mind.
The great question, my dear, is how one begins to attack
that state of mind. I wouldn't go so far as to say how to
overcome it. And in this sense New Guinea and the
Congo and even France become irrelevant, because we
are responsible for what is happening here. I'm not responsible for the Turkish or the Japanese societies, for
example. But I am in some way responsible for what happens here. I cannot change Japanese society.

MEAD: You sure can!

BALDWIN: Well, perhaps I can change it, but the price of
changing that society will be changing this one.

MEAD: But what we do has affected Japan.

BALDWIN: Yes, let me be reckless and go back to where we

really ended. I remember we were talking about the
South African miner and Western economy. Now, this
shirt I'm wearing, the dress you're wearing, it's not your
fault and it's not my fault, the price these rags cost the
world, but the economy is built so that it is standing on
the back of some nameless black miner in Johannesburg
and, as we said this morning, one day he will stand up.
What's on his back will crumble. What shall we do? We
cannot prevent his standing up. How can we minimize
the damage on him and on us?

MEAD: The damage on us when he stands up?

BALDWIN: Yes, because he will. How shall we manage that
day? The historical point of view will not help us then.
What you think and what I think will not help us then.
What matters is what we do now.

MEAD: Now, yes. Before then.

BALDWIN: What shall we do?

MEAD: Before then?

BALDWIN: What shall we do? How should we liberate that
man and us? Because that liberation is a double liberation. The life of my two-year-old great-nephew depends
on that liberation and so does the life of your children
depend on that liberation.

MEAD: Liberation.

BALDWIN: How should we achieve that liberation?

MEAD: Now, may I? I'm going to shift for a minute because
a piece of this—

BALDWIN: Yes, go on!

MEAD: It seems to me the kids who are denying history,
saying it's irrelevant, don't know anything about it.

BALDWIN: Well, kids don't know anything about history.

MEAD: They don't know enough to argue with adults. They
know things the adults don't know, but if they venture

into the field of history the adults will put them down
every time because they've been there.

BALDWIN: No, no. If I may interrupt you for a moment, you
used two difficult words here. Adults, it's a difficult word.

MEAD: Well, pre-World War II people.

BALDWIN: No, adults are rare.

MEAD: All right, grown-ups. You like that term? What are
you going to form—

BALDWIN: Adults are rare. Most people are grown-up children. And history is a concept that exists in nearly nobody's mind.

MEAD: Yes, but—

BALDWIN: Is that true or not?

MEAD: If you make it that way. I'm talking about something
else. The kids refuse to pay attention to anything that
happened before. They just say it's irrelevant; it doesn't
have anything to do with now. They say, We are talking
about now.

BALDWIN: What about Mr. Agnew?

MEAD: Mr. Agnew doesn't know any history, but he quotes
it. He doesn't refuse it; the kids do. They refuse it.

BALDWIN: Mr. Agnew, to use a very bad example—but we're
living in a rather bad example. I would go back to where I
was earlier. Luckily I'm not fifteen, but if I were and
listened to Spiro T. Agnew—and again I'm talking about
the office and not necessarily the man, *if* the man exists—
how in the world I achieve any respect for human life or
any sense of history by listening to that incredible example of self-satisfied vacuity who pretends to tell me who I
am? What I am trying to say is that if I were young I
would find myself with *no morals. Who wants to be Spiro
T. Agnew?*

MEAD: That's right.

BALDWIN: That's a very crucial situation. For that matter, who wants to be Georges Pompidou? Consider what we have done, our generation, the world that we have created. If I were fifteen I would feel hopeless, too. You see, what one has to do is try to face that the world is scarcely habitable for the conscious young. I read a little book called *The Way It Spozed to Be,* and it was poetry and things written by little black children, Mexican children, Puerto Rican children, from various schools in the land of the free and the home of the brave. And the teacher, who no longer was a teacher, made a compilation of the poetry these kids wrote and he let them talk. He respected them. He dealt with them as though they were—and in fact as all children are, as all human beings are—a kind of miracle. And because he did that, something happened. And for me that very tiny book . . . it's about thirty pages long. One sixteen-year-old boy who was in prison wrote a poem, and it ended with four lines I'll never forget: "Walk on water, walk on a leaf, hardest of all is walk on grief." What I'm getting at, I hope, is that there is tremendous national, global, moral waste.

MEAD: I know.

BALDWIN: And the question is, How can it be arrested? That's the enormous question. Look, you and I both are whatever we have become, and whatever happens to us now doesn't really matter. We're done. It's a matter of the curtain coming down eventually. But what should we do about the children? We are responsible; so far as we are responsible at all, our responsibility lies there, toward them. We have to assume that we are responsible for the future of the world.

MEAD: That's right.

BALDWIN: What shall we do? How should we begin it? How

can it be accomplished? How can one invest others with some hope?

MEAD: Then we come to a point where I would say it matters to know where we came from. That it matters to know the long, long road that we've come through. And this is the thing that gives me hope that we can go further.

BALDWIN: For that matter, it gives me hope, but I must speak in my own person, as Jimmy, and *you*, Margaret, cannot say that. I mean it cannot be heard, even by me, though I agree with you. And that's very important.

MEAD: Yes.

BALDWIN: I know what you mean and I agree with you, but people pay for what they do. Maybe I am an Old New England, Old Testament prophet. We were talking about guilt, before, and responsibility. I was really trying to talk about a dynamic that exists in time. And that painting on the wall reminds me of something that happened in the past—in time.

MEAD: That's Haiti, of course.

BALDWIN: Yes, but it doesn't make any difference. I took a boat to a small island called Garée, off the coast of Senegal, which is the nearest point on the Atlantic—the African West Coast—to America. I come from there, a tiny island with a great house on it, that house you saw in "Gone With the Wind." Two staircases. Beneath that staircase are the slave quarters. I walk through it with my sister. It's narrow and low and it's built of stone and it's wet. On either side of you there are the cells. The manacles are still there, rusted with time. For me, the smell is still there. And you're let out of that down this corridor, this stone corridor to the end of it. And the end of it is the Atlantic Ocean. Black stones at your feet and the sea foaming up and the horizon. And you are going where? Chained together, defecating together, sweating together, unable to speak to each other, going where? Now I, at the risk of being entirely romantic, think that is the crime which is spoken of in the Bible, the sin against the Holy Ghost which cannot be forgiven. And if that is true—

MEAD: Then we've nowhere to go.

BALDWIN: No, we have atonement.

MEAD: Not for the sin against the Holy Ghost.

BALDWIN: No?

MEAD: I mean, after all, you were once a theologian.

BALDWIN: I was once a preacher, yes indeed.

MEAD: And the point about the sin against the Holy Ghost is that—

BALDWIN: Is that it cannot be forgiven.

MEAD: So if you state a crime as impossible of forgiveness you've doomed everyone.

BALDWIN: No, I don't think I was as merciless as the Old Testament prophets. But I do agree with Malcolm X, that sin demands atonement.

MEAD: Whose sin? I mean, you're making racial guilt—

BALDWIN: No.

MEAD: *Yes.* You are.

BALDWIN: I'm not talking about race. I'm talking about the fact—

MEAD: But you are.

BALDWIN: I could talk equally about the English children dragging carts through mines—

MEAD: Yes, but you're—

BALDWIN: —before they got around to me.

MEAD: Yes, but you're being an Old Testament person.

BALDWIN: Prophet.

MEAD: You're taking an Old Testament position, that the sins of the fathers are visited on their children.

BALDWIN: They are.

MEAD: The consequences are visited on the children.

BALDWIN: It's the same thing, isn't it?

MEAD: No, it's not the same thing at all. Because it's one thing to say, All right, I'm suffering for what my fathers did—

BALDWIN: I don't mean that, I don't mean that! I don't mean that at all! I mean something else! I mean something which I may not be able to get to—

MEAD: Look, there have been millions of crimes committed against humanity. *Millions!* Now, why is one crime more important than another?

BALDWIN: No, my point precisely is that one crime is *not* more important than another and that *all* crimes must be atoned for.

MEAD: All right, *all* crimes.

BALDWIN: My little Jewish boy in that photograph, that dead little Jewish boy, is as important for me as my two-year-old great-nephew and the passage of the one hundred million.

MEAD: Yes, but when you talk about atonement you're talking about people who weren't *born* when this was committed.

BALDWIN: No, I mean the recognition of where one finds one's self in time or history or now. I mean the *recognition.* After all, I'm not guiltless, either. I sold my brothers or my sisters—

MEAD: When did you?

BALDWIN: Oh, a thousand years ago, it doesn't make any difference.

MEAD: It *does* make a difference. I think if one takes that position it's absolutely hopeless. I will *not* accept any guilt for what anybody else did. I *will* accept guilt for what I did myself.

BALDWIN: We agreed this morning that we had no right to be proud of our ancestors, but you could be proud of your child.

MEAD: That's right.

BALDWIN: And we agreed this morning that guilt and *responsibility* were not the same thing. But we have to agree, too, that we both have produced, all of us have produced, a system of reality which we cannot in any way whatever control; what we call history is perhaps a way of avoiding responsibility for what has happened, is happening, in time.

MEAD: If we can't control it, we're not guilty.

BALDWIN: But I'm not trying to make us guilty.

MEAD: Yes, you are. You're talking about atonement in one generation for the crimes of another generation.

BALDWIN: Let me put it another way, or let me *try* to put it another way. If something comes down in time, in that peculiar chemistry which we call time, it comes down from one person to another. There are lots of metaphors for it—ancestry, genealogy or whatever—it doesn't make any difference. Something does descend from generation to generation. In time. Is that true?

MEAD: Yes.

BALDWIN: Something does descend; we don't know what it is, really. But if that is so, I'm not talking about—really, I'm not talking about—guilt. I'm not trying to be Jeremiah. I'm only saying that at a certain point in one's own life—at a certain point in my own life—one has to accept the history which created you. And if you don't accept it, you cannot atone.

MEAD: No, but I don't see how one generation atones for what another generation did. It makes no sense to me whatsoever.

BALDWIN: Again in my own person, in my own person, it doesn't make any sense to me, either. That's not really the question. You had to be taught at some point, didn't you, that you were white? In any case, I had to discover that I was black.

MEAD: Yes, everybody in this country has to discover those things.

BALDWIN: Wait, wait! Then if that is so, all I'm saying is that I was born, and so are we all, carrying one's history on one's brow, whether one likes it or not. Whether you liked it or not, whether I liked it or not.

MEAD: To a degree.

BALDWIN: *No,* not to a degree.

MEAD: You're not carrying what your ancestors did a thousand years ago. You don't know—

BALDWIN: But that's a technical detail.

MEAD: Wait a minute. And if you take a good look you mightn't like it.

BALDWIN: Oh, I'm not being sentimental about that, either.

MEAD: And I'm not carrying what my ancestors did a thousand years ago, either.

BALDWIN: But you see, you are. We both are.

MEAD: No.

BALDWIN: I don't mean—

MEAD: I absolutely refuse that. I absolutely refuse racial *guilt.*

BALDWIN: I'm not talking about racial *guilt.*

MEAD: Well, it is. I mean, if a thousand years ago—

BALDWIN: Tsk, tsk, tsk. No, no, no.

MEAD: If I had an Irish bishop in the seventh century, an

Irish bishop who could have been my ancestor, because I had some Irish somewhere—

BALDWIN: Or mine.

MEAD: —who prayed that the Lord God would send a plague to kill off the lower orders because the earth was getting overcrowded—they did, a whole congregation of Irish Christian bishops—one of them could've been my ancestor, because I suppose they were . . . not all completely faithful to their vows.

BALDWIN: Then I'm being imprecise. I'm being imprecise. Let me try to put it another way. I'm not trying to accuse you or me.

MEAD: Well, one doesn't accuse a group of people, either.

BALDWIN: I'm not accusing a group of people, or you or me.

MEAD: But then you talk about it, a crime that was committed a long time ago.

BALDWIN: The crime that is committed until it is *accepted* that it was committed. If you don't accept, if I don't accept, whatever it is I have done—

MEAD: *You* have done.

BALDWIN: Whatever I, Jimmy Baldwin—

MEAD: In reality, that's right.

BALDWIN: If I don't accept whatever I, Jimmy Baldwin, have done, if I don't accept whether I love you or hate you, if I lie to myself about whatever it is I feel about anybody or about myself, then I'm trapped, aren't I?

MEAD: What *you* have done, yes.

BALDWIN: I'm doomed to do it forever. If I don't accept what I have done.

BALDWIN: What *you* have done, yes.

BALDWIN: If I don't accept what I, Jimmy, have done, whatever it is—it doesn't make any difference what it is—if I don't accept it I'm trapped in it. I will do it forever.

MEAD: But you're talking about yourself as an individual now, and in that I agree with you.

BALDWIN: Let me extrapolate, then. If that is true for an individual—if a person can be trapped in his crimes forever because he cannot admit his crimes to himself—then it must be true for civilizations.

MEAD: Civilizations aren't individuals, Jimmy. They're not individuals, they're not organisms.

BALDWIN: How do they distinguish them? How does a civilization distinguish from an individual? It's a loaded question.

MEAD: A civilization has been built by thousands of individuals whose responsibilities have been very different within it. And you can't—

BALDWIN: Are civilizations built by the individuals?

MEAD: Working together, unconsciously in most cases. They're built by great numbers of individuals, but not consciously.

BALDWIN: Then we're trapped in language, aren't we? Because the whole word *individual* implies consciousness.

MEAD: It doesn't to me; it just implies identity, not consciousness.

BALDWIN: Isn't that the same thing?

MEAD: No, any individual—

BALDWIN: When I decide that I am Jimmy, I know I am more or less conscious. I know I'm not Margaret.

MEAD: Do you know where you can find the absolute edge of individuality?

Baldwin: No.

MEAD: In a two-headed snake.

BALDWIN: Tell me about that.

MEAD: A two-headed snake, if it's bifurcated below or

above the stomach, knows whether or not it's an individual. If it has two stomachs, one head tries to eat the other.

BALDWIN: That sounds, alas, like the history of the human
race.

MEAD: No. Do you know where the human race has *come
from?*

BALDWIN: I don't know that.

MEAD: Do you have any sense of where it came from?

BALDWIN: I don't know that, but I know where it has not
gotten to.

MEAD: But of course not. Do you know that the estimate is
at present that the greatest brain that anyone has ever
known—

BALDWIN: But the brain—

MEAD: Well, wait a minute! Brains are a little useful every
once in a while. The estimate is that the greatest brain has
only used one tenth of its available potentiality. So we've
got nine tenths to go for the—

BALDWIN: We're foundering here in the morass of language.
I don't know what the brain means. I'm a very bright cat,
I'm told, but I don't trust that at all. If I'm bright at all,
and that's debatable . . . and I'm not kidding when I say
that. I'm not being coy or modest when I say that.

MEAD: It's *not* very debatable.

BALDWIN: It's very debatable to me.

MEAD: Well, permit somebody else to do the debating.

BALDWIN: I never learned anything through my mind. I
learned whatever I've learned from my heart and my guts.

MEAD: I know, but you can't translate what you learned in
your heart and your guts without your mind.

BALDWIN: You've got to get a pipeline from the bottom to
the top.

MEAD: That's right, and you need the top.

BALDWIN: But what may be called intelligence doesn't start in the mind, it starts in the heart and the guts.

MEAD: I don't think it matters where it starts so long as it goes through.

BALDWIN: But without a certain passion, and passion has no mind, without a certain love that—how can I put it, baby? Something has happened here and you have to feel it in your heart and your guts, and you have to feel a discipline to build that pipeline that brings it up to your mind.

MEAD: Yes.

BALDWIN: But if it doesn't start down there it doesn't mean anything. The world is full of bright people who are entirely irrelevant, and most of them are wicked.

MEAD: That doesn't change the fact that good, dumb people don't get very far.

BALDWIN: Most people don't love each other.

MEAD: But that is not the same argument.

BALDWIN: That is the most important thing; that is my argument.

MEAD: But it's not the same argument.

BALDWIN: I think that love is the only wisdom.

MEAD: Did you say early wisdom or only wisdom?

BALDWIN: Only wisdom.

MEAD: Maybe early wisdom would be a better phrase.

BALDWIN: Either/or.

MEAD: But an early, early wisdom.

BALDWIN: Either/or. Without that I don't think there is any hope for us, and there has to be hope as long as we're here. But I don't really think that in the brilliant zone your power and my power or anybody's power. . . . What makes you, for example, if I may be impertinent, the person that you are—we all know that you're brilliant —but what makes you really the lady with the marvelous face is that you earned it in some terrible crucible which is called life. You are a very beautiful woman, you really are. But you didn't earn it because you're bright.

MEAD: Well, but you see, there are things . . . there is a combination, I think—

BALDWIN: Yes.

MEAD: —that you're leaving out. There's a combination be-tween—

BALDWIN: Tell me about that.

MEAD: —the ability to *use* one's brain which I would prefer to say, instead of saying what kind of brain you have. Because nobody knows whether there's a real difference between the brain you have and—

BALDWIN: And the brain you get.

MEAD: Yes, but we know there's a great difference between the way people use their brains.

BALDWIN: That depends on life and the amount of the in-vestment you make in life.

MEAD: And it depends on how you learn.

BALDWIN: How you learn is how you feel, isn't it?

MEAD: Well, not only that.

BALDWIN: I didn't say *only*.

MEAD: But I think it's terribly important.

BALDWIN: Isn't that the key?

MEAD: No, I don't think so. I think there is something that is actually meaningful in the way you learn to think.

BALDWIN: Yes, but you learn to think because you're forced to learn to think, and you learn to think because you've *felt deeply enough* about something to think about it. Something happened to disturb the peace in you.

MEAD: If you can only count to twenty you can have all kinds of peace disturbed, but there is still a limit to what you can do, because you live in a culture where they can only count to twenty.

BALDWIN: Yes, yes, *d'accord, d'accord.*

MEAD: There are thousands of things that we've been saying in the last two days that nobody could have said—nobody, no matter how bright they were—two thousand years ago. They couldn't have said them no matter how bright they were.

BALDWIN: In one way, that's true. But, if I may, I must point out to you, or remind myself, that as a matter of absolute fact that is not true. The poets always said it.

MEAD: Well, from one point of view you can say that.

BALDWIN: A long time ago William Blake said, "A starving dog at his master's gate predicts the ruin of the state." That is as true now as it was then.

MEAD: Well, there are hundreds of things that were said ten thousand years ago by Eskimos that are true now, but there are a lot of things that one can say now that one couldn't say then.

BALDWIN: "Love thy neighbor as thyself." But what I'm saying is that there's always been . . . this is my act of faith, implicit in the fact of the human race. This is my commitment and yours. There's always been a knowledge much deeper than anything of which the mind informs us.

MEAD: Maybe, but do you know—

BALDWIN: That's why we have poets, and that's why Plato wanted them out of his republic.

MEAD: Right. But it wasn't until we got this extra bit of cortical ability—

BALDWIN: I agree. I agree with that.

MEAD: —that we knew what we had.

BALDWIN: Yes, but what I am trying to say—and I know we don't really disagree on this—is that now in the twentieth

century we are going to find only two terrible facts: the
fact of prose, on every single level from television to the
White House, and the fact of the hope of poetry, without
which nobody can live. I use poetry not in its most serious
sense.

MEAD: You know, I was trying to say—

BALDWIN: Do you know what I'm trying to say?

MEAD: Prose, or prophecies?

BALDWIN: Hey, maybe both. You know what I'm trying to
say, though?

MEAD: Yes.

BALDWIN: There's some faith in human nature, in what a
person can become no matter what time he's born in and
no matter what's behind him. We have to—in every generation, every five minutes—make human life possible.
That's the only importance of having a brain, because it's
a metaphor for stamina, isn't it? And finally it's a metaphor for love.

MEAD: I'm not arguing against any of this, but we're still
talking about time. That's where we started.

BALDWIN: Time, now.

MEAD: If you say, now. And this is what matters now, to
make human life—

BALDWIN: The only time we have is now.

MEAD: Right. But you keep talking about crimes in the past.
I still think you've got to dispose of them.

BALDWIN: My dear Dr. Mead. My dear Margaret. I will even
call you Mary.

MEAD: But not Dr. Mead.

BALDWIN: My point about it is that I don't think history is
the past. If it were the past, it would not matter.

MEAD: Ah, this is another way of doing it.

BALDWIN: History is the present.

MEAD: It's what we know about the past, but in the present.

BALDWIN: No, no, no. I don't mean that. I mean . . . what I was trying to say earlier . . . what I was trying to find out: How in the world is it that there are still anachronisms? If history were the past, history wouldn't matter. History is the *present,* the *present.* You and I are history. We carry our history. We act in our history.

MEAD: Okay. Half a million years.

BALDWIN: We *act* on it. And if one is going to change history —and we have to change history—we have to change ourselves because we *are* history. Do you see what I mean?

MEAD: I see what you mean, but I don't agree with you. You see, you can either say we are history because everything we know about ourselves . . . everything we know about ourselves is part of what we know now. Two hundred years ago we didn't know about evolution, so it wasn't part of people.

BALDWIN: I'm not convinced we know about evolution now.

MEAD: All right, but what we think we know about evolution now is part of us. What people thought they knew two hundred years ago was part of them. From that point of view, all of history is in the present and is operative now. That is one way of looking at it. But another way of looking at it is, of course, how much we are going to carry and take of what was and what we believe was.

BALDWIN: But according to me, what *was* is what *is.*

MEAD: What we *believe* was. Should we carry it on forever as a feud? For this is what it amounts to. It does!

BALDWIN: I don't mean that.

MEAD: Well, when you talk about it . . . Let's go back to that island, that point in Africa near Delmay—

BALDWIN: Garée, yes.

MEAD: —and your description of it. We're going to carry
   that on forever.

BALDWIN: I do not mean that at all. I mean that it happened.
   We were talking about time present and time past. I don't
   mean that at all. God knows, I'm not the least interested
   in carrying on the nightmare. Nevertheless, if I don't, if I,
   Jimmy, don't accept the very brutal facts of the past, then
   I have no present. I know that this brutality is not extraordinary. It's happened to everybody else in the world, too.
   I know that. But if I pretend that it did not happen to me,
   that I was not there, then I cannot live. That's what I
   mean by history being the present. I don't mean that I've
   got a bill to pay back or that—

MEAD: But you did use the word *atonement* and the term
   sin against the Holy Ghost.

BALDWIN: Yes.

MEAD: So it couldn't be forgotten.

BALDWIN: Let me say exactly what I mean by that. What I
   mean by that is if I, Jimmy, really offend you, Margaret,
   and I pretend I haven't, I have sealed my life off from all
   life, all light and all air. I will not get past my crime if I
   pretend I did not commit it.

MEAD: I agree with that about us.

BALDWIN: If I have offended you, I have to come to you and
   say, "I'm sorry, please forgive me." I'm only talking about
   that, and if I can't do that, then I cannot live. I'm not
   talking about crime and punishment.

MEAD: But you see, I agree with all this about you and me
   now and the children in the future. But if you take the
   past—

BALDWIN: But the past is the *present.*

MEAD: Wait a minute! My ancestors were hunted through

the caves of Scotland and tortured. Should I go back now and have a confrontation with Catholic Scots?

BALDWIN: I'm not talking about going back. Nobody can, anyway. The framework is the American civilization, isn't it?

MEAD: Yes, and my ancestors were hunted through caves before they got here. But I don't think it is particularly relevant, except for what I heard as a child.

BALDWIN: Yes, but my ancestors also had a curious history and were penalized and are penalized for it here.

MEAD: You're not penalized, Jimmy, for your history. No, you're not. What you're being penalized for is the ridiculous attitude—and you can find it in places with totally different histories—the European notion of superiority. You go to Israel today, you look at the German Jews, the German Jews who went to Israel and felt so infernally superior to everybody else there—

BALDWIN: Especially the Egyptians, the Algerians and the Yemenites.

MEAD: Exactly, all the "Asian" Jews. Now, this isn't about anybody being a slave. It isn't about this point; it's plain European superiority.

BALDWIN: But you're proving my point, my point being that history is not the past, it's the present. One may even make an argument, in a couple of more weeks, that history is never the past, that everyone is always acting out history. I watched, sitting on a café terrace in Tel Aviv. You sit there and you watch them; sitting on a café terrace in Tel Aviv, you see the Jews from every nation under heaven—one might even, indeed, call them, in the Biblical sense, a Remnant, though this Jewish state was created by the West, for Western purposes, not out of any love for Jews or any sense of atonement; this is a Jewish

state created by England for England's purposes—you
see the Russian Jews, the German Jews, the English Jews,
and those are Europeans. You see the Egyptian Jews, the
Algerian Jews, and those are not Europeans. And they do
not mix with each other, in spite of the fact that Israel
considers itself a religious state. No matter what the
Christian motives were in creating the state, the Jews are
there as Jews. And all of them look down on the
Yemenites, and that is history in the present, isn't it?

MEAD: This is *life* in the present.

BALDWIN: A Russian Jew walking through Tel Aviv is not a
figure in the past. He is carrying his history with him and
acting it out. So is the Algerian Jew.

MEAD: And so is the Yemenite.

BALDWIN: All of them. It is *not* yesterday's history. It is *now*.
If that were not so, we couldn't hope to change history.
For this is what I'm demanding.

MEAD: Then it seems to me what you do. . . . So you're
the Yemenite. Let's stay in Israel for a moment.

BALDWIN: I am the Yemenite.

MEAD: You're the Yemenite. You're not a Yemenite now,
just—

BALDWIN: Oh, I dance and sing as well as the Yemenites do
and pay the same price for it.

MEAD: And can you balance parchment on your knee and
write so perfectly, and if you're asked why you don't have
a table you say it's not sturdy enough.

BALDWIN: How do you think I became a writer?

MEAD: Not by balancing parchment on your knee like a
Yemenite. All right, you're all in Israel together, all these
different groups.

BALDWIN: Not together.

MEAD: Well, yes, in many ways.

BALDWIN: Physically together, if you like. You know, the way one's together at a cocktail party.

MEAD: It's true they haven't quite made it in Israel. But it's a lot better than a cocktail party, Jimmy.

BALDWIN: Tsk, tsk, tsk.

MEAD: Oh, yes, it is.

BALDWIN: I was in Israel several times and watched it very carefully. They are *not* together.

MEAD: The European Jews didn't do too well, but nevertheless they tried. Now, to the extent that each one of them carries with them an attitude that is distilled from the past, I would say the past is there. You take those—

BALDWIN: Then you're agreeing with me: the past is present.

MEAD: Wait a minute! A lot of the past is present. But what I'm interested in is what then do we do with it? Now if—

BALDWIN: I think we can't do anything with it until we understand that the past is the present. And we can't change the past, but we have to change the present. Or, we can only redeem the past by what we do in the present.

MEAD: Well, we've got a big problem there, because a lot of people are trying to change the past right now, and you've really got a—

BALDWIN: We're trying to change the past. We're trying to change the present. The price for that is our apprehension, our acceptance, of the past. I don't care what other people are doing. I care what you and I are doing.

MEAD: A lot of people try to change the present by changing the past.

BALDWIN: No, no. I'm not romantic about history at all.

MEAD: Do you think it's important to use what we think at present, by documentation, is so?

BALDWIN: What we think at present is not so very important.

MEAD: Well, you just said that we are only living in the present.

BALDWIN: What we think at present?

MEAD: All right, believe me, I don't care. Look, the point is: Suppose we believe that the Battle of Waterloo was fought and it influences the French and all the things that happened, all right? So does it matter whether it was fought or not?

BALDWIN: No, it doesn't. But it does matter what you make of it.

MEAD: It doesn't matter whether it was fought or not?

BALDWIN: Well, let me put it this way. It does matter because it was a very crucial event in the history of Europe. But you could also say, in the imagination of Europe.

MEAD: That is, it did affect subsequent events.

BALDWIN: It does.

MEAD: It *did*. If it didn't, it wouldn't *does*.

BALDWIN: It does.

MEAD: Yes.

BALDWIN: We have no argument here, you know. We have no argument here.

MEAD: I think we do.

BALDWIN: What's the argument?

MEAD: I think there is a real difference between believing that something—

BALDWIN: Believing in what will happen?

MEAD: No, believing that something *did* happen.

BALDWIN: Like the virgin birth?

MEAD: Well, like the virgin birth, if you like. It makes a great deal of difference whether you believe the virgin birth happened or not.

BALDWIN: Yes, but did it?

MEAD: That is another problem. And that is not resolvable, but we do—

BALDWIN: That is my point.

MEAD: But the existence of the Battle of Waterloo is resolvable, at least by the tests we have of what did happen.

BALDWIN: Like the retreat from Moscow. Insofar as the virgin birth and the retreat from Moscow and the Battle of Waterloo did happen or did not happen to the extent that anyone alive believes that they happened, they're controlled by that belief, and that means that history is the present.

MEAD: I'm perfectly willing to agree with you, but there is a difference.

BALDWIN: Between the virgin birth and the Battle of Waterloo.

MEAD: Yes, that's point one. Point two, the whole of the West at present bases its position—its whole position, really—on the fact. . . . For instance, if there had been cameras at the Battle of Waterloo, they could have taken pictures of it and we could have developed the film afterwards. Whereas in India you have the phenomenon of a woman who gives evidence at a trial and the trial is appealed. Then she gives different evidence, totally different evidence, and the British-trained Indian lawyer says to her, "But you can't do that; you said this and now you say that. Now one or the other is so; you can't change your evidence like that." She says, "But I am not the same person."

BALDWIN: Oh, that's wild. That's really wild. But it's not all that mysterious.

MEAD: That is an Asian position. And these are fundamentally very different positions.

BALDWIN: You know *Porgy and Bess?*

MEAD: Yes.

BALDWIN: There's a moment in *Porgy and Bess*—

MEAD: About the divorce?

BALDWIN: —which is not my favorite opera. No, no.

MEAD: There's a wonderful bit about getting a divorce when you haven't been married; that's very relevant.

BALDWIN: There's one line in there which is the only line that is really true about American blacks, perhaps about the orientals. The cops come to look for Porgy. Everybody in Catfish Row knows exactly who and where Porgy is, and the cops come and say, "Where's Porgy?" and the line is, "Porgy? I don't know no Porgy. Do you know Porgy?" They never find him.

   This connects with what I was trying to say earlier about the great gap between white and black life styles here. You come looking for my brother. I don't care what he's done or what I *know* he's done. I don't *care*. I may kill him, but you won't. You'll never find him, not from me. That is where we are. That is where we are! This extraordinary Republic has created this extraordinary division which is now global.

MEAD: When you say it's now global . . . but once we weren't even there.

BALDWIN: Yes, but history is the present.

MEAD: And what we make of it. If I—

BALDWIN: That is up to you and me, isn't it?

MEAD: That's right, and if I can convince people that we've come a terrifically long way—

BALDWIN: But you won't be able to convince me for a very long time to tell you where Porgy is.

MEAD: But I don't want to ask you. You have to weed that out. I don't want you to tell me where Porgy is.

BALDWIN: I know that, Margaret.

MEAD: I only want you to realize things about other people.

BALDWIN: Let me tell you something else. I think I do realize some things about other people. Maybe what I realize is more bitter than I would like it to be. I realize that. I was thinking about it all day long, and when this rather terrifying show is over, I'll come and have a drink with you without any microphones or anything, because I want us to be friends and you know I mean that.

MEAD: Yes.

BALDWIN: But I was thinking about time, or history, all day long. And I thought, It is quite true, quite true—the necessity for the long view. But I have no right; my history, if you like, doesn't give me the right. . . . I know that two thousand years ago . . . I know, I know, I know, I know, I know, I know. But a man's life doesn't encompass even half a thousand years. And whether or not I like it, I am responsible for something which is happening *now* and I must bear witness to what I know *now* and fight as hard as I can for the life of everybody on this planet now.

MEAD: I agree.

BALDWIN: Do you know what I mean?

MEAD: I agree, and the thing I wanted to talk about earlier, when you started about time, is the more one wants to be an activist the narrower the time is.

BALDWIN: Precisely! Precisely! I said we have no argument.

MEAD: What the kids say . . . if you cut out all the past—

BALDWIN: You can't.

MEAD: Wait a minute! They do. And it permits them to act in the present as they could never act if they had to stop and have an argument.

BALDWIN: As a matter of fact those kids, to deal with those kids for a minute, are not acting in the present at all; they are acting in the past. They don't know it. It takes a long time to realize that there is a past. It takes a long time, you know. If I decided to blow up a bank at twenty and decided to blow it up at forty, that's a very great difference. A kid can't look back over twenty adult years, and to the extent that he doesn't have any past, he's trapped in it. Those kids are romantic, not even revolutionaries. At least not yet. They don't know what revolution entails. They think everything is happening in the present. They think they are the present. They think that nothing ever happened before in the whole history of the world.

MEAD: That maybe gives them a kind of strength.

BALDWIN: Oh, no, baby.

MEAD: Oh, yes, right in line with what we have been saying. Because the more you narrow it, the more strength you have to act.

BALDWIN: No, no, no. I don't believe that either. I think that the act of narrowing it is a very self-conscious act. To think it's narrow is one thing, and to narrow it deliberately is another. You have to be forty to narrow it. Nobody narrows it at twenty. They can't. They can't see back. There's nothing to look back on.

MEAD: There again, you're taking in a sense the individual as a kind of model.

BALDWIN: But I'm a poet.

MEAD: Yes, but I'm not.

BALDWIN: Oh, I don't agree with you. I don't think that's true. I think that you and I, for example, have met and understand each other and are committed to each other because we really, no matter what the terms may be, have the same commitment. And that commitment is to the human race.

MEAD: But I don't think that makes one a poet.

BALDWIN: That *is* what makes you a poet.

MEAD: See, I think what makes you—

BALDWIN: And there's nothing you can do about that.

MEAD: I acknowledge the commitment and I think also we have mainly communicated in poetry. You see, all the conversation that we've been having is primarily this poetic communication. It's not prose, it's poetry.

BALDWIN: But that's very important, isn't it?

MEAD: Sure, it's poetry and not prose. But I'm not a good poet.

BALDWIN: Neither am I, but I am a poet. I'm saying it really for me. It's very difficult for me to say I am a poet. I don't mean anything about my talent, whatever it may be. That has nothing to do with it. I'm not vain about those things at all. There's far too much to learn, so many things to do. I'm talking about a certain kind of responsibility. And there's only one responsibility and that is really toward the future, however mystical that may sound.

MEAD: No, I agree.

BALDWIN: One, is a commitment to generations unborn. That is what it is all about. And I don't care what word one uses, poetry or prose; it doesn't make any difference. That commitment is very, very rare, and we cannot fail each other because whatever it is you have or whatever it is I have does not belong to you or to me. It belongs to all of us.

MEAD: Yes.

BALDWIN: We are meant to be witnesses to a possibility which we will not live to see, but we have to bring it out. It has nothing to do with you and nothing to do with me. It has to do with what we know human beings have been and can become, and that is so subversive that it is called poetry. Check with Plato.

MEAD: Yes, checking with Plato, that would be so. But Plato
was not a poet.

BALDWIN: That's why he didn't want any poets in his republic. It took me a long time to understand that, a long time.
But he described poets as disturbers of the peace.

MEAD: Yes.

BALDWIN: And it took me a long time before I realized what
he meant by that. But that's exactly what you are, aren't
you?

MEAD: A disturber of the peace.

BALDWIN: And that peace has always got to be disturbed.
That's the point; that's what's meant by the angels trou-
bling the waters. Right?

MEAD: Right.

BALDWIN: Okay? I'm having fun, if you don't mind.

MEAD: Of course I don't mind.

BALDWIN: Great!

MEAD: If we start off with this commitment to the future
and the unborn, and these are the people that we hold in
our arms—

BALDWIN: Tightly or with the back side of the other arm.

MEAD: That's right, but we hold them—then what we make
of the past is what we give them as part of the future. The
thing I object to is taking the past where, at different
times over the history of man, one group has wronged
another. If we went over it enough, every group has
wronged every other at some point or another or somewhere. If we perpetuate this—and I think that this is
quite different from acknowledging the facts and is the
reason I came back to the facts—there are two things that
can be done. One thing you can do is to produce the
rather fantastic versions of the crucifixion that people will
write: for example, saying that another people were in-

volved or Jesus was not crucified or one of these things. You can build any kind of a structure that you want. And a great many people in the world are very busy building new structures out of the past to nourish them in the future.

BALDWIN: You mean new myths.

MEAD: New myths. I think there's a difference, and this is where I am a Westerner.

BALDWIN: So am I.

MEAD: And so are you. And I think that one of the things that frees us is to find out what did happen and face what did happen. And that means that white America has to face exactly what did happen and, of course, black America has to face what did happen. Now, my definition of what did happen is that if there'd have been a camera there running on its own steam with no human being to press the button on or off what would have been on the film is what really happened. Now this is a philosophical point, and it makes a lot of difference.

BALDWIN: I follow you.

MEAD: What did happen does make a difference to me, and if you deny that order of evidence—

BALDWIN: But, Margaret, I don't deny that at all.

MEAD: When you accept the past that's what you mean?

BALDWIN: Let us even go further than that. I mean to use the past to create the present. I really don't have any interest in accusing anybody alive of anything. For that matter, I'm more terrified of black cops than I am of white cops. And I'm not sentimental in that way, I don't think, at all. What I'm trying to say is what you just said, really. From my point of view, we have to take the past and find out to what extent the things one carries in one's self—the burdens we carry out of the past—cause you to do what we call the past. That burden we all carry in the present; one has to discover to what extent your apprehension of the past dictates the shape of the future.

MEAD: I agree with all of that, but we still have to decide whether one is going to attempt to see that one's apprehension of the past is related to what, in quotes as I'm defining it, "did happen," or whether it's to be a view of the past that is completely constructed. There's a film running around now called *A Man Called Horse*. Have you seen it?

BALDWIN: No, I stopped going to the movies.

MEAD: Absolutely beastly. It was made to make money only.

BALDWIN: This is all about history and the present.

MEAD: But it's using American Indians. It has an Englishman, a beautiful blond Englishman—

BALDWIN: Who else?

MEAD: —who comes out among the Indians, and only by becoming as cruel as they are—

BALDWIN: As cruel as who is?

MEAD: The Indians. And those particular Indians were cruel.

BALDWIN: Those Indians were cruel?

MEAD: Many American Indians were cruel, now this is a fact.

BALDWIN: If they were, they are.

MEAD: No, no, because their children are something else again. But what he does . . . what this picture says is the way to make friends . . . if you translated this into a paradigm for the future, the way in which the white man in America can understand the Indian—this is Indians today: Navahos who are hungry and Pueblo Indians who have pine needles for vitamins; Indians today who are living people—the only way that he can be one with them is to be as cruel as their ancestors were, in a different context, a totally different context, long ago.

BALDWIN: But, my dear, isn't that—?

MEAD: Which I think is horrible.

BALDWIN: Isn't that an example of the dream reversed? Isn't that a kind of confession of how oblique is our reading of history? The kind of confession you get in a nightmare of what you know you have done?

MEAD: No, you see, I do not accept that I have done things because I dreamt about them.

BALDWIN: But I had to accept that I was on a slave boat once.

MEAD: No.

BALDWIN: But I was.

MEAD: Wait, you were not. Look, you don't believe in reincarnation?

BALDWIN: But my whole life was defined by my history.

MEAD: All right, my life was defined at some point a hundred thousand years ago when I was a pre-hominid.

BALDWIN: No, my life was defined by the time I was five by the history written on my brow.

MEAD: This is a question of where you slice history!

BALDWIN: No, no, *no, no, no!* We're talking about a five-year-old boy who knows nothing about history, who comes into the world and who finds himself paying for it because everyone else can read his history, though he cannot.

MEAD: What?

BALDWIN: It didn't happen a thousand years ago in another country. It happened to me *here*.

MEAD: All right.

BALDWIN: Because I was here.

MEAD: If you make this as the only point—

BALDWIN: I'm not making it. I didn't make it. It is not my
idea, not my invention. I'm telling you a fact. There's
nothing you can do. It's nothing that I did or didn't do.
You didn't know. . . . When I was ten years old—I'm
very small now; when I was ten I was much, much smaller
—two cops who were not ten *beat* me half to *death*. Now,
what was speaking there, me or my history? Them or
their history? How can I claim history as the past if two
grown men—two grown men, not one—committed a hei-
nous crime on a black boy because he's black? I don't
want to hear about a thousand years ago or even fifty. I
was ten and nearly died because of history written in the
color of my skin. That's a fact which no one can get
around. God knows I can't. I don't want to pay anybody
back for it. I'm not being vengeful, but it is a fact. And
according to me, that's the central fact in the history of
my country which, however odd it may sound, I love. And
until one faces that fact, faces that great wreckage, that
pile of corpses, we are all being murdered, we are murdered in many, many ways: some with the fire bright;
some with a rope; some by the river; some, you know, just
castrated; some dead while they live. I'm sorry; I'm an
Old Testament prophet—and that is a sin.

MEAD: The Africans rewrote their history every year because it was oral, so they could. Today Africa lives in the
future. And Israel lives in the future. I've stood on a
mountain and seen them look at a university that wasn't
built, but they see it all there.

BALDWIN: Yes, but Margaret, Margaret, we cannot avoid the
question of power. Let me be very cynical.

MEAD: Cynicism is the other thing that goes with sentimentality, you know.

BALDWIN: I know. Let me be very cynical and point out to

you that from my point of view, not only from my point of
view, five British mandates, five successive British mandates, promised land equally back and forth to the Arabs
and the Jews, didn't they? That is not from my point of
view, that's a matter of history, it's a matter of record. We
do know that millions and millions and millions of Jews
were murdered, sometimes in the harbors of friendly nations, because no one would take them in. Is that true or
not?

MEAD: I think so, yes. I'm not sure about millions, but—

BALDWIN: Millions. It doesn't make any difference. One.

MEAD: Okay, I agree with you. It doesn't make any difference whether—

BALDWIN: And we do know that Israel is in the Middle East
and that's a very important part of the world, isn't it?
Well, that's a matter of public record, and from my point
of view the creation of the State of Israel was one of the
most cynical achievements, really murderous, merciless,
ugliest, and cynical achievements, on the part of the
Western nations. They don't care about the Jews.

MEAD: But it could not have happened without the Jewish
dream.

BALDWIN: Wait a minute. Wait a minute! *Wait a minute!*
The British didn't care about the Jews.

MEAD: Jews didn't care about other people either.

BALDWIN: That is not, at the moment, my point.

MEAD: You know that it's relevant.

BALDWIN: I agree with you. But the creation of the State of
Israel was not for the sake of the Jews. It was for the sake
of—

MEAD: The fact that the Jews got Israel was not for the sake
of—

BALDWIN: They didn't get Israel. It was given to them.

MEAD: Well, I know. But, it wouldn't have been given to them if they hadn't been working for it.

BALDWIN: It was given to them because it was useful for us, for the West. We put a handful of people at the gate of the Middle East, in an entirely hostile, embattled area where they could be murdered at any moment and we knew it, not because we loved the Jews but because we could use them.

MEAD: And because the promoters of Zionism could use the British. Remember, those were parallel points.

BALDWIN: I remember the Merchant of Venice, too.

MEAD: *Really?*

BALDWIN: Yes! The Jew was still doing the Christian's dirty work. I am not accusing the Jews when I say that, but it is extraordinary that an entirely irreligious people should reclaim land after three thousand years, because of texts in the Bible, and displace forty million people. Or how many, I don't even know how many.

MEAD: I don't think—

BALDWIN: Because of something that is written down by Jehovah on a tablet?

MEAD: I don't think— This is so inconsistent!

BALDWIN: Why?

MEAD: You have to give your thoughts of Israel right back to—

BALDWIN: I am against the State of Israel.

MEAD: Well, I am not!

BALDWIN: I don't mean I am against the Jews when I say that. I mean I am against the State of Israel because I think a great injustice has been done to the Arabs. There is no defense for their situation. I was there.

MEAD: I have been there, too, you know!

BALDWIN: I was there and I know something, if I may say so,

both for better and for worse about American Jews. That's a terrible phrase to use, but it is the only phrase I can use now.

MEAD: You better say Jewish Americans.

BALDWIN: American Jews: Jewish Americans. It doesn't make a difference.

MEAD: Now wait a minute, we had an argument we dealt with before—

BALDWIN: Jewish Americans. Actually, the term is up to them. You have got to remember, however bitter this may sound, no matter how bitter I may sound, that I have been, in America, the Arab at the hands of the Jews.

MEAD: Oh, fiddlesticks! Tut, tut, tut. Just plain fiddlesticks! You are now making a totally racist comment, just because there have been a bunch of Jewish shopkeepers in Harlem.

BALDWIN: Wait a minute. Wait a minute.

MEAD: Yes, you are.

BALDWIN: No, I am not.

MEAD: I suggest we drop this because it gets us nowhere and will get us nowhere. These are just a set of imperfectly realized analogies. Frankly, it will get us nowhere.

BALDWIN: Wait a minute.

MEAD: I will have nothing to do with it. Nothing to do with it.

BALDWIN: Wait a minute.

MEAD: I am not a racist.

BALDWIN: There was a doctor named Dr. Meyer, who was our best friend in Harlem.

MEAD: Look, anecdotes—

BALDWIN: Wait a minute! Wait a minute!

MEAD: Look, Jimmy, I could write every word you are going to say, and I am not interested.

BALDWIN: No, you can't!

MEAD: I bet I could!

BALDWIN: Let us not try to avoid it. There were several Jews in Harlem, of course, but there was one doctor who took care of us for nothing, for years, until he died. And we loved that man. There was a man across the street who gave us food for nothing, for years, until he died. And we loved that man.

MEAD: *But—*

BALDWIN: I have not said "but."

MEAD: Well, you are going to.

BALDWIN: I have not said "but."

MEAD: Not yet.

BALDWIN: I have not said "but." I have not said "but."

MEAD: But you are working up to it.

BALDWIN: No, I am not. Don't despair. Wait a minute. I'm serious. I really am serious. Because that means it was one of the greatest crises in my whole life. This whole Jewish/black thing. I really know—

MEAD: Don't blame the Jews for your religious youth.

BALDWIN: I am not talking about that at all. Now you force me to go down to the end of the story. I must tell you, therefore, this. I didn't know that Dr. Meyer was a Jew. I just knew he was white and I liked him. I didn't know that Leroy was a Jew, the man who owned the grocery store. I just knew he was white and I liked him. He liked me and I liked him. I knew he fed us. I didn't know that the man who owned the apartment and wanted the rent was a Jew, and I hated him. They were all white to me.

MEAD: *Yeah.*

BALDWIN: It didn't make any difference. I didn't know what a Jew was. It didn't make any difference to me *at all!* I knew the way he treated my mother and I loved people according to the way they treated my mother, my father, my brothers and my sisters. And that was all I knew and I didn't care. The Jewish thing did not enter into my calculations until much, much later, when my father, who hated Jews. . . . For him all white people were Jews. I was too young to understand that either. I had a Jewish friend, my best friend. That's a very banal thing for an American to say, but my very best friend was a Jew.

MEAD: And you brought him over and your father didn't like him.

BALDWIN: And my father beat the shit out of me. It taught me something. I can say what I say about American Jews or Jewish Americans because I love them, or at least loved one. That's the same thing. And I learned from some of the people who loved me enough to save me. It was that Jewish boy in high school who got me out of the church, and that demanded a tremendous act of love. You know, I am not talking about those things on that level.

MEAD: But—

BALDWIN: There is no "but."

MEAD: But there is a "but," because we are getting the—

BALDWIN: Well then, the "but" is that the Jewish American, the Italian American, the Greek American, the Yugoslavian American—anyway, all white Americans—all came to America probably to become Americans, and the price for becoming an American, the badge, is very much like being Indian and having a white man's scalp. In this case, it is my scalp. And it is not the color of the skin that matters, it is the custom of the country. That is true.

MEAD: There again, you see, you are going back into the past.

BALDWIN: I am not going back into the past. I am only forty-six years old and we are in New York. When I go downstairs out of this building I can be murdered for trying to get a cab. That is not the past. That's the present.

MEAD: Let's consider for a moment another image of the Negro that the white man once held. This was that the Negro stood for someone who was happier, happy-go-lucky, enjoyed life more, didn't go to work when it rained. You know the whole story that—

BALDWIN: The syndrome.

MEAD: No, the whole picture that John Dollard quotes in *Caste and Class*.

BALDWIN: Yes.

MEAD: You know, the mother who says, "All you children would have been black if I hadn't gotten behind on my insurance." That is, "I never would have had anything to do with a white man except for economic reasons." Now, there are those who say that the puritanical complex in this country is being relaxed and people don't feel they have to work all day long, all the time, so they're going to take over the role of enjoying life which was once the thing that they projected on the Negro, and the Negro, like the Jew, is going to suffer more. Now, I don't believe in this entirely because it has not happened yet. But it is curious, and it is true of European history, that as long as the Christian was not allowed to lend money, Jews were tolerated and treated fairly well in Europe.

BALDWIN: Well, that's what I meant when I said that the Jews were still doing the Christians' dirty work. For example, in Harlem, the man who owns the building in which you live—

MEAD: You know, this isn't true in the United States anymore.

BALDWIN: It's true.

MEAD: Oh, fiddlesticks!

BALDWIN: No, Margaret, I was there.

MEAD: Look, the Jews owned it.

BALDWIN: The Jew was a landlord, but the Christian owned the land; the Christian owned the building.

MEAD: Sometimes and sometimes not.

BALDWIN: The man who owned the building—

MEAD: It may have been Trinity Church, I know, but I—

BALDWIN: Precisely. The man who owned the building did not arrive to collect the rent. The Jew was the middle-man.

MEAD: Or Columbia University. Or Syrians.

BALDWIN: It doesn't make any difference.

MEAD: Wait. Wait. It does make a difference. These are the kind of facts that make a difference.

BALDWIN: In our case it was the Jew.

MEAD: Yep, I know, but you said—

BALDWIN: Now, I know this is a very dangerous conversation, and let me try to clean it up a little bit. I don't want to get sidetracked on anti-Semitism. My only point is a very simple one: That before the American Jew or the Jewish American is a Jew he is an American, like anybody else in this country, and the crisis for me is whether or not we will be able to overcome the uses to which we have been put and become something resembling a people, instead of several tribes, because that is what we still are.

MEAD: If you had ever seen a real tribe, you wouldn't talk about a tribe in the United States.

BALDWIN: I have.

MEAD: I mean—

BALDWIN: Well, that depends.

MEAD: Aggregations, temporary aggregations.

BALDWIN: At the risk of being a bore, let me say one last

thing because I think it is very important—not for me or for you, necessarily, as Margaret Mead and Jimmy Baldwin, but it is very important for whatever it is one hopes to do. I may be wrong, you know, I may be fanatical, I may be deluded, but I have to talk out of the only thing I have, which is my experience. And my experience beside the golden door for forty-six years—and I will not live another forty-six years; and I am speaking to you also as a world-famous man—has been so bitter that I cannot, have not yet been able to, begin to describe it. And not bitter merely for me, bitter enough for me, a cup that nobody should ever have had to drink. But what is bitter is the incomprehension of your co-citizens.

I walked out of a New York cocktail party, the literary cocktail party scene, a little over ten years ago because I had a fight with a taxi driver about one of my brothers. I do have three brothers who are not famous but at the mercy of any cop. I spent a fortune, fortunes and fortunes and fortunes, calling up New York from Paris or wherever I was whenever niggers were in the streets. I know what I am talking about. I really do.

MEAD: I know that.

BALDWIN: Wait a minute. One of my brothers was in trouble, and I was at this cocktail party and a very famous American intellectual—I wasn't talking about my brother because I don't do that; I was trying to say something about my country, and he said to me, "What are you crying about, Jimmy? You've made it." I could not believe I heard him. Made what? He told me a lot about what he thought he'd made and a lot about my country and I walked out and never went back and never will. Because something in me despises that level of ambition. Made

what? A Cadillac? A house? An air-conditioned nightmare?

MEAD: You don't like air conditioning?

BALDWIN: I don't think that I have the right to settle for it,
because my brothers and my sisters have paid too much
and are paying too much to live in this terrifying country.

I know that other countries are terrifying, too. I am not
romantic. I have been in lots of places. I don't pretend
that any place else is any better. But I am responsible for
this particular place and this particular time, and my
brothers are not historical figures. They are not going to
live forever, any more than you are or I am, and I think
one is responsible to those lives. It is in that sense, I
think, that one transforms the world and makes history
something one can live with. You know what I am trying
to say?

MEAD: But you see, I agree with all of this. I completely
understand this and agree with it. And you have another
little problem here to cope with, and that is that in a
sense I have never suffered as you have.

BALDWIN: That's not true.

MEAD: I am sorry, it is.

BALDWIN: Oh, no.

MEAD: In the terms you are discussing, it is completely true.
I was born in a family where I was the child— Wait a
minute! Now just stop making faces and let me talk for a
while. I was a child that both my parents wanted. I had
the traits that they liked, that each one of them liked in
the other. I was told from the time I was born that I was
totally satisfactory. I had a chance to be what I wanted to
be and I have always been able to be what I wanted to be.
I don't like Cadillacs, either. And I don't own one. I don't
even own a fur coat. But nevertheless, because I was born

where I was, I was fortunate. And it wasn't only because I was white, because there are an extraordinary number of white people in this country who are born very unfortunately. I might have been very unfortunate had I been the third child of my parents instead of the first, with a baby who died in between somewhere so my father decided that he was never going to love the younger children too much.

But I have got to talk to you, you see, and I think that this is a problem. It isn't only race. It is weighted by race, oh, it's weighted by race. So you give yourself the same father and the same mother but you grow up in a small Iowa town. Fifty percent, seventy-five percent, God knows how much of suffering you would not have had, see? I mean, you just think of the things that you suffered by, and most of them were created by Harlem. Now, your father. If you had had your father as a father but he had been white. . . . He could have been, you know. There have been white preachers that were just as rigid as your father.

BALDWIN: But not for quite the same reasons.

MEAD: Yes, that's right. And the reasons themselves make a difference, you see. So, although you could have had many of the same experiences if you transformed your family—and you could transform a lot of it into a white community and make yourself white—when you did you would take away a great deal of the suffering.

Now, you see, it seems to me this is so: that a large amount of the things that have happened to you, that have filled you with fury and commitment, have been because of color; one doesn't deny that. But you see, you have got an odd problem with me because the reason I've been happy is not because of color.

There is an asymmetry here. It wasn't because I was sitting vis-à-vis black people, being privileged, as has happened in many parts of the world. I didn't belong to a separate class. I lived in a small Pennsylvania community and I was brought up with tremendous concern for every person who was poor or different in that community. In a sense my happiness was a function of the fact that my mother did insist that I call the black woman who worked for us *Mrs.* My felicity was a function of a denial, if you like, or a refusal of a caste position. Your suffering was a function of the fact that a caste position was forced on you. And they are not symmetrical, they are not symmetrical.

BALDWIN: I agree. I agree that there is an asymmetry. And I don't want to make a contest between your felicity and my unhappiness because I am not, first of all, talking about either your felicity or my unhappiness.

MEAD: Yes, but I think we have to deal with it. Because you have dealt in your writing over and over again with the situations in your life. You have dealt with them because it illuminated the situation of black people in America or in the world, which is terribly significant to illuminate.

BALDWIN: I wish I could illuminate the position of the white people in the world.

MEAD: Certainly. But you see, there are two kinds of positions with white people in the world. If you have a caste position . . . if I had been living in the South, or in most American northern cities, or if I had been a child of most white Americans, I couldn't—

BALDWIN: You're proving my point again.

MEAD: Wait a minute. I could not have had the degree of felicity I have had.

BALDWIN: Yes, but you are proving my point.

MEAD: Yes, I am proving it, except it has got to be somehow clearly stated.

BALDWIN: Look, we are both—

MEAD: You see, I could go anywhere in the world. I can take any people in my arms.

BALDWIN: *You* can!

MEAD: I have. We are dealing with—

BALDWIN: We are both exiles.

MEAD: No, I am not an exile when as an American I go abroad. I am not an exile.

BALDWIN: I am an exile. But I was an exile long before I went away. Because the terms—this is the point, for me —the terms on which my life was offered to me in my country were—

MEAD: Weren't good enough.

BALDWIN: No, not good enough, entirely intolerable and un- acceptable.

MEAD: Right.

BALDWIN: My country drove me out. The Americans drove me out of my country.

MEAD: But you have never left in spirit. I mean, when you are at work and when you write your writing on behalf—

BALDWIN: That is a matter of stamina, luck and pride.

MEAD: Well, and belief, isn't? Faith.

BALDWIN: Hope.

MEAD: Yes. Hope.

BALDWIN: But the fact is that I am an exile because I can't live in America under terms on which Americans offer me my life. And that says something about my country and nothing at all about me.

MEAD: You know, I don't think you can say anything about your country without saying something about yourself, too. Because lots of exiles leave and really leave.

BALDWIN: I left because I wanted to live.

MEAD: But you also left at the same time you wanted to remain an American. You could have become a citizen of another country. You don't want to because you acknowledge the fact that this is your country.

BALDWIN: No.

MEAD: However badly it treats you.

BALDWIN: No, no, let me be honest. I am not so sure of that. I am *not* so sure of that. I am *not* so sure. I told a little girl once at a lecture—a little black girl about ten years old who said, "My teacher says I refused to salute the American flag. Do you think I was right or wrong?"—I told her, "I am going to pledge allegiance to any flag which pledges allegiance to me. Otherwise you are a beggar, and I am not a beggar."

MEAD: This is just what my people in New Guinea said. After the war all taxes were abolished. And then my New Guinea people elected to pay taxes because they said, "Otherwise we cry to the government, and we don't want to cry to the government. We will pay taxes and ask for what is our right."

BALDWIN: We did that on a famous day in Washington. I was there.

MEAD: You mean when Martin Luther King gave the "I have a dream" speech?

BALDWIN: Yes. And do you know the answer we got? Two weeks later, ten days later, after that enormous petition? You know the first answer that the Republic gave us? My phone rang one morning—I was back in Hollywood, God knows why—and a CORE worker was telling me, she could hardly talk, that four black girls had been bombed into eternity in a Sunday school in Birmingham. That was the answer the Republic gave!

MEAD: But you see, I would say that the Republic did not give that answer, because I am part of the Republic and I didn't give it.

BALDWIN: I am not accusing you.

MEAD: Wait a minute.

BALDWIN: I am accusing the Republic.

MEAD: What's the Republic? You can't accuse an entity like the Republic.

BALDWIN: My countrymen.

MEAD: In what is a conquered nation, the Old South. Now wait a minute! You see, this is the—

BALDWIN: My countrymen.

MEAD: Which countrymen?

BALDWIN: My countrymen.

MEAD: All of them?

BALDWIN: All of them.

MEAD: All right. That includes me.

BALDWIN: It includes me, too!

MEAD: Did you bomb those little girls in Birmingham?

BALDWIN: I'm responsible for it. I didn't stop it.

MEAD: Why are you responsible? Didn't you try to stop it? Hadn't you been working?

BALDWIN: It doesn't make any difference what one's tried.

MEAD: Of course it makes a difference what one's tried.

BALDWIN: No, not really.

MEAD: This is the fundamental difference. You are talking like a member of the Russian Orthodox Church. You are talking exactly like a Russian Orthodox. "We are all guilty. Because some man suffers, we are all murderers."

BALDWIN: No, no, no. We are all responsible.

MEAD: Look, you are not responsible.

BALDWIN: That blood is also on my hands.

MEAD: Why?

BALDWIN: Because I didn't stop it.

MEAD: Is the blood of somebody who is dying in Burma today on your hands?

BALDWIN: Yes, yes.

MEAD: Because you didn't stop that? That's what I mean by the Russian Orthodox position, that all of us are guilty of all that has been done or thought—

BALDWIN: Yes.

MEAD: And I will not accept it. I will not.

BALDWIN: "For whom the bell tolls."

MEAD: I will not.

BALDWIN: "For whom the bell tolls."

MEAD: No. That is different. "And therefore never send to know for whom the bell tolls, it tolls for thee" means I am *concerned* with the suffering of everyone in the world.

BALDWIN: No. It doesn't mean that. It means everybody's suffering is mine.

MEAD: Everybody's suffering is mine but not everybody's murdering, and that is a very different point. I would accept everybody's sufferings. I do not distinguish for one moment whether my child is in danger or a child in Central Asia. But I will not accept responsibility for what other people do because I happen to belong to that nation or that race or that religion. I do not believe in guilt by association.

BALDWIN: But, Margaret, I have to accept it. I have to accept it because I am a black man in the world and I am not only in America. I find myself in France or I find myself in Egypt, it does not matter where I find myself. It doesn't make any difference. I am identified whether I like it or not, like a German during the epoch of the Third Reich, with Senator McCarthy, the late-lamented, with Ronald Reagan, with Vietnam. I have a green passport

and I am an American citizen, and the crimes of this
Republic, whether or not I am guilty of them, I am responsible for.

MEAD: But you see, I think there is a difference. I am glad I
am an American because I think we can do more harm
than any other country on this earth at the moment, so I
would rather be inside the country that could do the most
harm.

BALDWIN: In the eye of the hurricane.

MEAD: In the eye of the hurricane, because I think I may be
able to do more good there. You know, it would be very
pleasant to be a Dane. It's a nice little country. But what
one could do as a Dane—there are a lot of things you can
do as a Dane, you know—but, nevertheless, the Danes
can't do much harm to the world. The Danes can do
some good but they can't do much harm. This country
can do incredible harm or incredible good.

BALDWIN: What do you mean *can* do?

MEAD: Look, there are a lot of other countries doing a lot of
harm, too.

BALDWIN: I am not responsible for those countries.

MEAD: You were talking as if one should be responsible for
the whole human race, the way you are talking. You say
somebody was murdering on the steppes of Asia, it's your
fault; you are a human being too.

BALDWIN: I told you before, I am a poet.

MEAD: Yes, I know. But still, as a poet, you decide whether
you are going to take the human race on or only America.

BALDWIN: Who has founded America? Not the entire human race?

MEAD: No, not the entire. . . . No Australian aborigines
here.

BALDWIN: All right, all right.

MEAD: No, we don't represent the whole world.

BALDWIN: With one or two exceptions.

MEAD: Yes. One or two exceptions. But you said before, one makes history now. I am worried if you have to have a different functioning in the world, a different definition of responsibility, for a black man and for a white man. You see, I would like to feel, and maybe it isn't true, but I would like to feel that it would be possible—as you and I agree that the only thing that matters is the future—that we are responsible for that. That we are responsible for those unborn children, black, white, yellow, red—green, as the Seventh-Day Adventists say—all of them. We agree completely on that.

Now, is it necessary at this moment in history—and say the next ten years—for someone who is black to take a different stance in relation to the past although we take the same stance in relation to the future? Now it may be. You see, the question I was raising earlier is that maybe in order to act one has to take a different stance.

BALDWIN: Margaret, Margaret, Margaret. Not so very long ago I had to go visit some people in prison in my country. I sat in the waiting room. You know who is in jail in my country. From California to New York. I know what is happening in my country and I think I know why. It is not a question of my point of view. I have sat there and I know that we are being murdered and nobody cares. Now, a thousand years from now it will not matter; that is perfectly true. A thousand years ago it was worse; that is perfectly true. I am not responsible for that. I am responsible for now.

MEAD: Now.

BALDWIN: And what is happening in my country *now* is unacceptable to me. And if it has to go under in flames, that is too bad. I will go with it, but I won't accept it. I will *not* accept it.

MEAD: Yes, but what is the difference between when you say you won't accept it and I say I will work to change it? I mean, you live in Paris and I live here, but what is the other difference?

BALDWIN: Well, I am driven out of here. When you say you won't accept it, it comes to the same thing. But what I am trying to convey, really, I suppose . . . we talked earlier—

MEAD: Maybe it is different, you see.

BALDWIN: No. When we talked earlier about poverty and rage . . . I am one of the dispossessed. There is that difference. According to the West I have no history. There is that difference. I have had to wrest my identity out of the jaws of the West. It's a very different endeavor. We, the blacks, have been told nothing but lies. So have you been told nothing but lies.

MEAD: That's right. We have both been told lies.

BALDWIN: But there is a difference in that you—

MEAD: Whether one was the lied about or not.

BALDWIN: —you are identified with the angels, and I'm identified with the devil. We are living in a kind of theology. Therefore my situation—our situation, really—presents itself to me as exceedingly urgent. I cannot lie to myself about some things. I cannot. I don't mean anybody else is. I mean that I have to know something about myself and my countrymen, and the most terrible thing about that, the most terrible thing about it, is not the looting, the fire burnings or the bombings: that is bad enough. But what is really terrible is to face the fact that you cannot trust your countrymen. That you cannot trust them. For the assumptions on which *they* live are anti-

thetical to any hope *you* may have to live. It is a terrible
omen when you see an American flag on somebody else's
car and realize that's your enemy. In principle it is your
flag too, but the man who is flying the American flag is
going to kill you. You, his brother. You, his countryman.
That is what that flag means. Ask Southeast Asia if you
doubt me. That is a bitter, bitter, bitter pill, but it is like
that.

MEAD: I am not denying any of these facts. What I am trying to consider is whether there is an inevitable difference in the spiritual stance, for you who are black and me
who am white.

BALDWIN: We can't talk about the spiritual stance unless we
are talking about power!

MEAD: All right, so I am the color of the people who have
power here. So if we went to British Guiana, where you
are the color of people who have power, would the thing
change?

BALDWIN: British Guiana has no power. You know that as
well as I do.

MEAD: Well, it was in that—

BALDWIN: That is why it is called British Guiana.

MEAD: Well, within that country, within that country, we
have a reversal between black and brown and white.

BALDWIN: That country does not exist!

MEAD: You mean it is not big enough?

BALDWIN: I mean it does not exist.

MEAD: What do you mean, it does not exist?

BALDWIN: The Guinea dite. La Guinea, according to the
British.

MEAD: Look, I am talking about British Guiana in South
America.

BALDWIN: Yes. But you say "British Guiana in South Amer-

ica." But South America. . . . Why is it called South
America?

MEAD: Well, I still say British Guiana not Guyana as it is
today because I am ancient.

BALDWIN: No, it is not because you are ancient. It is because—

MEAD: Oh, yes, it is. Because I am distinguishing it from
Dutch Guiana.

BALDWIN: Well, you are proving my point again! I am talking
about the resentment of the people who are called British—

MEAD: All right, they should be called Guyanians.

BALDWIN: —who are not British, and people who are called
Portuguese who are not Portuguese.

MEAD: You are now going back on everything you have said.

BALDWIN: All right, all right.

MEAD: You are, completely. I mean, what made that country? East Indians dragged over from India and from Indo-
nesia. Africans from Africa, and a few British from England. And who put it together, and what is the language?
The language is English and they do stem back to Britain.
And you said—

BALDWIN: The language in fact is not English. If one really
examines the language spoken, it is an English which died
with Queen Victoria.

MEAD: Look, you are just going back, Jimmy, on all the
things you said earlier. You said earlier that you grew up
here, you spoke English; you're an American. All right. I
say the people who grew up in Guyana grew up within a
British tradition; they speak English. And you don't like
this. Now, why not? What made that country?

BALDWIN: The British. The British system of law, and the
French system of law. The European system of law in

Africa was a legal means, it *is* a legal means, of administering injustice. When I said to you earlier—

Look, how can I put this? I have a certain relationship to someone, let us say, in British Guiana, and my relationship to him dictates that I chop off his head for reasons hidden to the Europeans. Now there is a way to try me. But you cannot possibly know what I have done nor why I have done it if you think of me as a savage.

MEAD: I don't know what we are talking about now.

BALDWIN: I am talking about—

MEAD: I am talking about a *particular* country.

BALDWIN: I am talking about . . . I am talking about power.

MEAD: I know, and I am talking about a country where the power is in the hands of black people. And I want to know—

BALDWIN: It is not.

MEAD: Oh, fiddlesticks, it is.

BALDWIN: It is not.

MEAD: Who do you think?

BALDWIN: In no country in Africa is the power in the hands of the black people.

MEAD: I keep telling you I am not talking about Africa. I am talking about a country in South America—

BALDWIN: Called British Guiana.

MEAD: That's right. It was its old name and it is now called Guyana and it is not in Africa.

BALDWIN: It doesn't make any difference.

MEAD: I am sorry, Jimmy, you are now going into symbolism that does not get us anywhere. You are just making speeches.

BALDWIN: I am not, I am not. There is an island called St. Croix—I was there a couple of years ago—which be-

longed to the Danes. It doesn't any longer belong to the
Danes, but it still belongs to Europe. Everybody on that
island had to refer to another authority.

MEAD: The Virgin Islands are of course completely dependent on the United States. They are part of this country.

BALDWIN: That does not make any difference. The people
on the island don't like being called by Danish names.
The people in Guyana don't like being called British Gui-
anans.

MEAD: They want to be called Guyanians.

BALDWIN: They want to be called by whatever their name is,
and they have to find that out for themselves. I am talking
about power. I am talking about that South African miner
on whom the entire life of the Western world is based.

MEAD: Well, I'm just sorry, because it isn't only based on
that South African miner. It is based on miners in this
country and miners in Britain who are underground.

BALDWIN: It is the same principle.

MEAD: It isn't the same principle as long as you are going to
continually make it racial.

BALDWIN: I am not being racial.

MEAD: You *are* being racial. I present you with human situations and you make them racial.

BALDWIN: Charles Dickens talked about the kids being
dragged through mines long before they discovered me.

MEAD: That's right.

BALDWIN: We are talking about the profit motive.

MEAD: We were? Look, you said there is a difference in
power. I said okay, and you reversed it.

BALDWIN: Look, let me put it this way—

MEAD: What I feel is this. We agree that we are both Americans. We agree in the sense of responsibility for the present and the future. You have approached this present

moment by one route and I have approached it by another. In the colors of our skin you represent a course of victimization and suffering and exploitation and everything in the world. If you just use skin color, I represent the group that was in the ascendance, were the conquerors, had the power, owned the land—you can say anything you like. All right. Now here we both are. Now, furthermore, I do not represent and I never have been a part in the whole of my life, because of the accident of my upbringing and so forth, of the kind of psychology that would perpetuate this. You also have moved around, have lived in many parts of the world, and although you completely understand what happens here you have included a lot of other things in your psyche. Now is it necessary for you to narrow history down and express only despair or bitterness while I express hope? Is this intrinsic to our position at the moment? Or can both of us out of such a different past and such a different experience—a contemporarily different experience because you in your own country, wherever you go, are likely to meet with insult, with indignity—

BALDWIN: Danger.

MEAD: Yes. Whereas wherever I go, on the whole—if they have not heard me say I was in favor of repealing the laws against marijuana—I am greeted with, on the whole, courtesy and kindness. So that contemporaneously your experience and mine will continue to be different. Now, given that fact can we both, nevertheless, stand shoulder to shoulder, a continent or an ocean away, working for the same future? I think this is the real problem.

BALDWIN: I don't think that is the problem.

MEAD: Or do we have to work on it differently?

BALDWIN: I don't think that is the problem at all. I take that, your supposition about being shoulder to shoulder, as a fact.

MEAD: Well, suppose you state why you think it is a possible fact.

BALDWIN: I don't think it is a possible fact. I think it is a fact.

MEAD: You think it is a fact. Okay.

BALDWIN: You see, we are trying to be precise about two different things which are not so different when they are examined. I am the history of America. My history in this country also says a great deal about this country. In fact, our histories put side by side—

MEAD: Four or seven or eight generations.

BALDWIN: —are the history of this country.

MEAD: That's right. The old history.

BALDWIN: Well, you have got to make it new. You see, what I am trying to say . . . I am not really talking about the past. This situation is very much like poor late Martin.

MEAD: Like what?

BALDWIN: Poor late Martin . . . Luther . . . King. And I am, too. You know, the question you have thrown at me is not my question.

MEAD: But I think this is an important question. You know I am not Lillian Smith.

BALDWIN: I didn't think you were.

MEAD: I know. Of course you didn't; I don't mean that. But in this country the dialogue between white and black has usually been with Lillian Smith representing the whites. Someone who has had a sort of conversion from a position that was originally antithetical. The fortunate thing is that I was never in that position. I have never been in the position of believing that I had any rights because I was white. I have been in the position of acting out white supremacy in New Guinea to save everybody's lives, because I was in a situation where it was necessary. But I never felt one moment of white supremacy in New Guinea, and I simply do not have the feeling which is one component in this country. So I am in an odd position. You know you have several times mentioned suffering. I don't think that I have any claim to any suffering, because I don't think either sympathy or empathy are real suffering. Real suffering is when the iron is on your own flesh. No matter how much you care about the people who have the iron on their flesh, if you don't have it on your own you don't suffer. I have never suffered in the sense that we are talking about here. Never. And we can include Women's Liberation, too. I have never suffered. But the reason I haven't suffered—and this is the one sort of thing that we can think about—is because as a child I was lifted out of the situation that grips this country and is destroying it. I was lifted out of it as a child. I was never permitted to grow up in it, and neither was my own child ever permitted to grow up in it, because I saw from the moment that she was born that she received loving kindness from both black and white people and so they were all people to her. They meant something to her.

So you and I are in some ways well matched, because we have both worked and we have both written and we both have some reputation for having written. And I think we are well matched as human beings. But what I think needs to be somehow resolved is how to deal. . . . I mean, is the person who would work better with you in this dialogue—I am not proposing to give it up; don't get kittens—but is the person who would work better with you someone who had grown up with all the scars of white supremacy? Because I agree with you that the oppressor and the oppressed both suffer and they are both scarred. One suffers more than the other, but the oppressor is probably far more scarred morally than the oppressed. Now, we could have had a conversation here with one person representing the scarred oppressor—

Wait a minute! We could; they do exist. They get converted, and the only way you can have a conversation with a scarred oppressor is after they get converted. So there are plenty of them in the world, someone who came out of the white world that had lived and built its dignity and built its sense of identity on the fact it wasn't black, the way males in this country build their sense of superiority over the fact that they are not female. Now, that is a conceivable conversation. It isn't the conversation that is being held, because I have neither been scarred nor specially benefited by being white.

BALDWIN: Yes, but you see, *there is an area where we both were exiled.* You said you weren't, but you are because of what you know.

MEAD: I am what?

BALDWIN: An exile—

MEAD: Oh, no, I am not.

BALDWIN: —from the mainstream of the life in this country.

MEAD: I am not an exile. I am absolutely not an exile. I live here and I live in Samoa and I live in New Guinea. I live everywhere on this planet that I have ever been, and I am no exile.

BALDWIN: What you mean is that you refuse to accept the condition of being an exile.

MEAD: I what?

BALDWIN: You refuse to accept the condition.

MEAD: No. It is just not—it really isn't meaningful to me to say that. I am not an exile. I accept the condition of man, the condition of man at this present state and the condi-

tion of man where I live and the point of greatest responsibility for that, but I am no exile. I am at home.

BALDWIN: I can't say that.

MEAD: No, you can't say this. You know, this is one of the
dramatic points of difference.

BALDWIN: I am not at home. I am not at home.

MEAD: Anywhere on this planet?

BALDWIN: Forever.

MEAD: Hmmm.

BALDWIN: Forever. I am not like you in one way.

MEAD: Can you think of a world—

BALDWIN: No.

MEAD: —in the future where you would be at home?

BALDWIN: No. The future doesn't exist for me.

MEAD: But it could change your present if you could think
of it.

BALDWIN: No, no, no. I am not romantic. I am not romantic.
I am not at home here and never will be. That means that
I will never, never, never, as long as I live, be at home
anywhere in the world.

MEAD: Because you are not at home here?

BALDWIN: Because my countrymen have rejected me. Or
the experience which created me.

MEAD: Then you would have to start with your own feeling—

BALDWIN: And the terms of their acceptance are terms that I
will not accept. No power under heaven or under the sea
or beneath hell will ever allow me to take my place in this
particular pantheon. I reject it in toto, with its virgin birth
to the alabaster Christ, in toto. Because it has brought
nothing but death and misery to me and mine.

MEAD: How—

BALDWIN: I intend to change it.

MEAD: But how?

BALDWIN: I don't know yet.

MEAD: You see, that is the next question.

BALDWIN: Ah! That is the question I live with. But the first step is to say no. And I have said no. No. I will not accept it.

MEAD: Then, if one transforms your no, which you have given geographical form to, to a no inside the country, because everybody can't move to Paris—

BALDWIN: Yes, but that no, my no—

MEAD: Your no is underwritten by your success.

BALDWIN: Oh, no.

MEAD: Oh, yes, it is.

BALDWIN: Oh, no.

MEAD: All right, Jimmy. Suppose if you had money—

BALDWIN: I don't have any money, in fact.

MEAD: I know. But you can make money.

BALDWIN: Oh, but I always could.

MEAD: All right, but not the kind of money that would take you to live in another country.

BALDWIN: I got to Paris with forty dollars and no French.

MEAD: I know, but—

BALDWIN: It wasn't money.

MEAD: You couldn't continue to live abroad without money. Your living abroad is a function of your writing for this country and because this country wants to read it and buy it. Now let us face that because you are living abroad.

BALDWIN: Let's face it. Let's face this—

MEAD: You are being allowed to be an exile because what you say matters here.

BALDWIN: Let's face this—

MEAD: Now what are people going to be? What are they

going to do after they read your saying you are rejecting it all? What are they going to do? They can't go to Paris.

BALDWIN: They could learn to live. . . . Oh, I see what you mean.

MEAD: They can't go to Paris. You are talking to them. We are talking for Americans here first.

BALDWIN: Not really.

MEAD: Oh, yes, we are. Or at least I am. I am not speaking—

BALDWIN: I am not so concerned—

MEAD: —for Koreans.

BALDWIN: I am not so concerned anymore—

MEAD: Hmmm.

BALDWIN: I am not really so concerned about Americans. If they don't know they exist yet, then that is their problem. And, if you look at it from my point of view for a moment, you would see that I cannot afford to be concerned about, however brutal this may sound—

MEAD: About what?

BALDWIN: My murderers. Because this country, my country-men, are my murderers. And that has nothing to do with my point of view. Nothing to do with whether I am neu-rotic or not.

MEAD: It doesn't?

BALDWIN: *That* is a fact. They murdered nearly all my friends and menace everybody left, and that is a fact. From my point of view, America does not matter so very much.

MEAD: What does?

BALDWIN: Mexico matters.

MEAD: You think—

BALDWIN: Vietnam matters.

MEAD: You think that Mexico and Vietnam can save the world? I mean for the future?

BALDWIN: I know that we will not.

MEAD: Well, if we don't save it—

BALDWIN: We won't.

MEAD: Jimmy, if we don't save it we will destroy it.

BALDWIN: We won't. My point precisely.

MEAD: And Mexico and Vietnam will have nothing to do with it.

BALDWIN: My point precisely.

MEAD: All right. You are saying, then, the world is going to be destroyed; there is no use doing anything about it?

BALDWIN: No. I don't intend to be passive. But America will not save us.

MEAD: But you see, we're . . . America—

BALDWIN: America doesn't know enough about the world. America doesn't know anything about you.

MEAD: Look, neither does Russia.

BALDWIN: *I am not Russian!*

MEAD: Look, you just said you were not too worried about America, but let's recognize you are.

BALDWIN: I said America does not matter so much because it *cannot* do and *will not* do what it has promised the world to do. It did not give me forty acres and a mule; it did not honor the treaties that it made with the Indians. *It has told nothing but lies, all over the world, to everybody in the world!*

MEAD: Just like every other imperial power.

BALDWIN: I do not belong to any other nation.

MEAD: Okay, but—

BALDWIN: This is my country. *And I am accusing it of being not only my murderers but yours too!*

MEAD: This is a thing I cannot agree with. If I were—

BALDWIN: But you were not born in Harlem; you didn't shine shoes with me.

MEAD: *Wait a minute!* Okay? This is just what I am saying. This is what I am saying is the issue. That if I connived in any way in thought, word or deed—

BALDWIN: Margaret, this has nothing to do with you or me.

MEAD: Look, you said earlier that the only thing that mattered . . . we must measure in terms of ourselves and not—

BALDWIN: We said responsibility is not guilt, did we not? I am not guilty of having sold myself onto that boat which got me here. You are not guilty of having starved out the Irish nation. But we are responsible—

MEAD: For the future. For the present and the future.

BALDWIN: If we don't manage the present there will be no future.

MEAD: Yes, that's right.

BALDWIN: And I have lost. . . . I must put it this way, really. There was a time in my life not so very long ago that I believed, hoped—and I suppose hope falls with believed—that this country could become what it has always presented as what it wanted to become. But I am sorry, no matter how this may sound; when Martin was murdered for me that hope ended.

MEAD: You know, because we all heard the speech he made, he knew he was going to be murdered.

BALDWIN: Yes, I know he did.

MEAD: And I don't believe he felt that was an end.

BALDWIN: I know he didn't.

MEAD: I believe he felt—

BALDWIN: It doesn't make it less unforgivable.

MEAD: Wait a minute.

BALDWIN: It doesn't make it more forgivable.

MEAD: Wait a minute. The Christian message, and it was one he believed in, was that God so loved the world he gave his only begotten son that all who believed in him might not perish but attain everlasting life. Now, however one interprets the Christian message, supernaturally or naturally, what it's meant to man through history was a God who loved mankind enough to take on human flesh and suffer for their sake—which is what Martin believed.

BALDWIN: I know he did. But you must concede, I think, that the Christian God—

MEAD: I don't think of a God . . . I don't think of God in terms of any race or any religion.

BALDWIN: No, but—

MEAD: But that particular point is related to what Martin believed.

BALDWIN: I will agree with it. It doesn't make any difference whether I agree or not. It really doesn't. Martin was extraordinary. Some people say deluded, but it doesn't make any difference whether he was deluded or not. He believed what he believed, and he paid for it with his life. Yet according to the Christian theology, God created him but not in his image.

MEAD: No, no.

BALDWIN: That is what the *Christians* have always told me.

MEAD: No, it is not what the Christians have always said. After all, the early Christians back in the Middle East didn't say this. There've been perversions—

BALDWIN: I wasn't there among the early Christians in the Middle East.

MEAD: That's right.

BALDWIN: But I was on those cattle boats which brought me here, brought me here in the name of Jesus Christ.

MEAD: No, Jimmy, no.

BALDWIN: In the name of Jesus Christ.

MEAD: No, they didn't bring you here in the—

BALDWIN: In the name of Jesus Christ.

MEAD: They did *not* bring you here in the name of Jesus Christ! That is a perversion.

BALDWIN: One of the boats was called "The Good Ship Jesus."

MEAD: Look, in New Guinea too we have copra bags stamped with "The Sacred Heart of Jesus Limited" because the mission filled them.

BALDWIN: Let's not go—

MEAD: "The Sacred Heart of Jesus, Limited."

BALDWIN: Let's not go into that.

MEAD: No.

BALDWIN: Let's not go into that. All I am saying is that the Western world will either live by what it professes to believe in or it will cease to exist.

MEAD: Yes, but you see what I'm saying—

BALDWIN: I'm not looking forward to the end of it, since I'm—

MEAD: You *can't* look forward to the end of *it*. You can only look forward to the end of *everyone*.

BALDWIN: I know that.

MEAD: But that is what you're not quite facing.

BALDWIN: Or I look forward to my own end.

MEAD: Look, Jimmy, you keep—

BALDWIN: When this ship goes down I go with it.

MEAD: I know you may go with it but you have—

BALDWIN: What do you mean *may?*

MEAD: Yes, because you're in Paris.

BALDWIN: Tsk, tsk, tsk. Paris is a friendly nation.

MEAD: I know, but you keep talking about the possibility that the Western world, if it doesn't meet its ethic of the present, will go down. It's not that. It will go down; the whole planet will go down.

BALDWIN: That may happen.

MEAD: You see, it is crucial at the present moment in history. What the Western world does is crucial.

BALDWIN: You say history, I say time.

MEAD: All right, the present time. I'm very willing to say either one. But it just happens that either the United States or the Soviet Union, and possibly rather soon China, could destroy the entire planet. This is crucial if we want the future for those children. If we want this nephew of yours, of whom you speak so movingly and identify with the future of all children. It is crucial for my granddaughter. If we want them to live it is absolutely essential that we recognize that the Soviet Union and the United States, either one of them, could destroy the world, and that we are not going to have a world made up of Mexico and Vietnam with Russia and the United States eliminated. It's unrealistic. The change has got to occur here, within this country and within the Soviet Union and in China.

BALDWIN: But it won't.

MEAD: Well—

BALDWIN: It won't.

MEAD: Then why do you stay alive one day?

BALDWIN: Well, some people come after it.

MEAD: Not on this planet.

BALDWIN: America is not about to change.

MEAD: Not on this planet then. I mean, if America doesn't change—

BALDWIN: I'm a member of the human race, and I know that America will not change, however paradoxical that may

sound, however contradictory that may sound. This ignorant people—

MEAD: And so you—

BALDWIN: —has yet to discover—

MEAD: *And so you contribute to its not changing!* That's
what you're doing now, you see. Not in your earlier
books, but now you're contributing to its not changing
and to the destruction of all human life on this planet.

BALDWIN: No.

MEAD: Yes, you are.

BALDWIN: I don't think so.

MEAD: Well, you mean you think if—

BALDWIN: I cannot be deluded by the people whom I know
best of all the people on the earth.

MEAD: Do you think if you tell them they won't change,
they will? Are you just trying to provoke them into better
behavior?

BALDWIN: Allen Ginsberg said, "Don't call the cop a pig, call
him a friend. If you call him a friend, he'll act like a
friend." I know more about cops than that.

MEAD: Which cops?

BALDWIN: All the cops.

MEAD: You don't know anything about the young college
people who are becoming cops today.

BALDWIN: I know a lot about the colleges.

MEAD: I'm sorry. You don't know! You don't know a thing in
the world about the young college people who are going
into a tough situation with a tough ethos, trying to change
it.

BALDWIN: Uh huh, uh huh.

MEAD: And what you know about the colleges is not relevant.

BALDWIN: What I do know is that I do not like to be corralled. I don't like being a subject nation. That I do know.

MEAD: Yes, you know what—

BALDWIN: And I don't care *how* well the cops are educated. I know what their role is in my life, and I will not accept it.

MEAD: Yes, but how are you going to change it?

BALDWIN: Blow it up.

MEAD: That changes nothing.

BALDWIN: I don't care what happens.

MEAD: You turn into a cop just like them after you've blown everything up.

BALDWIN: I know that, too. Still, I know that my situation cannot be endured. It cannot be endured.

MEAD: But what—

BALDWIN: And if I turn into a monster by trying to change it, that is a risk my soul will have to take. I'm not being objective.

MEAD: No, I don't think you should be.

BALDWIN: I'm trying to say this—

MEAD: I don't think I'm being objective either.

BALDWIN: No, I know you're not. You shouldn't be.

MEAD: I'm speaking out of the passion of what I believe in.

BALDWIN: Yes. Precisely. Now, we've got to make some kind of connection between what you believe and what I've endured. I'm not using you as Margaret or me as Jimmy. But you really must consider seriously, I think, the state of a nation in which I, Jimmy, or I, historically, am forced to say I do not care what the pursuant facts are. I cannot afford to care.

MEAD: But you see, the significant thing is that sentence: "I cannot afford to care." That's what I've been talking about all along. That maybe you *can't* afford to care and I can. Now, what is the difference between the people who cannot afford to care about the facts and those who can? And that's a real difference.

BALDWIN: The difference is that you, generically, historically, write the facts which I am expected to believe. The difference is that you, historically, generically, have betrayed me so often and lied to me so long that no number of facts according to you will ever convince me.

MEAD: If that's so, the world is doomed. If we can't reach a point where everybody *in this world can understand facts*. . . . See, that's it—

BALDWIN: But that's not.

MEAD: —about me.

BALDWIN: But I'm talking to you.

MEAD: Wait, I know—

BALDWIN: Which is the best the country at the moment can afford. You don't exist in this country either.

MEAD: Oh, yes, I do.

BALDWIN: Any more than I do.

MEAD: Oh, yes, I do. Jimmy, that won't go.

BALDWIN: Well—

MEAD: That won't go, that just won't go.

BALDWIN: Let me put it another way. You and I are both in the same very difficult hot seat. America doesn't want you any more than it wants me.

MEAD: Jimmy, it isn't true. We've got to face the fact that isn't true.

BALDWIN: Oh! You think I'm popular here?

MEAD: No, but I *am*.

BALDWIN: You think so?

MEAD: Yes.

BALDWIN: Well, you're tough.

MEAD: No, I belong here, you know.

BALDWIN: So do I.

MEAD: I know, but you at the moment feel your belonging-
ness is nonexistent, so you take a different stance. Now,
we've got to face that fact and we've got to face the fact
that you say truth will never matter to you anymore.

BALDWIN: I didn't say truth, I said facts.

MEAD: Well, facts. But remember that when I'm talking I'm
talking about actuality. I've defined what I mean.

BALDWIN: But you don't write *Time* magazine.

MEAD: Jimmy, that's not what we're talking about.

BALDWIN: You said facts.

MEAD: I'm talking about real facts. I'm not talking about
Time magazine. It's often inaccurate.

BALDWIN: To put it mildly.

MEAD: All right, but this is not what we're talking about.
We're saying. . . . It seems to me, your key sentence
there was "I cannot afford—

BALDWIN: No, I can't.

MEAD: —to care about the facts."

BALDWIN: No, I cannot afford to believe you. I don't mean
you.

MEAD: All right. Wait a minute! The real issue is, Can you
afford to believe me?

BALDWIN: I do believe—

MEAD: Wait a minute! Just consider this for a minute.

BALDWIN: I do believe you.

MEAD: Not can you afford to believe *Time* magazine, can
you afford to believe me? Now maybe you can't, you see.
I mean I think this is a real issue.

BALDWIN: Yes, I see what you are saying. Let me say this. In
nothing that we've done in these last—what?—forty-eight
hours or whatever it was . . . if I did not believe you,
you, you, I couldn't talk to you at all.

MEAD: But isn't that the answer?

BALDWIN: Wait a moment. That's the beginning of the question. I, Jimmy, trust you with me and mine. I'm not talking about that at all. I am talking about the state of the nation.

MEAD: But don't you think this is part of the state of the nation? That you can trust me even though you have shaken the dust of the country off your feet?

BALDWIN: It is. Oh, I will never be able to shake the dust of this city off my feet. I'm not romantic, as I said before. I have a lot of work to do, and I have to find a way of doing it. That's my problem and nobody else's, because there are no excuses. If I have to go to Tokyo to do it or find a cave to do it, I have to do it and I'll find a way to do it. It doesn't make any difference where I find it or what I do as long as I do it. That is all that matters there. You know I trust you. That is not the point. The country doesn't trust you or me. That is the point.

MEAD: You see, I don't think that's true.

BALDWIN: Well, well.

MEAD: You see, I don't think it's true.

BALDWIN: Well—

MEAD: There are enormous—

BALDWIN: Well, well.

MEAD: —groups in this country that trust you and trust me.

BALDWIN: Well, well, that may be enough to save the country.

MEAD: And maybe not.

BALDWIN: But it's very slim. We've agreed, haven't we? That's all I'm trying to say.

MEAD: But it's worth trying.

BALDWIN: Look, I also breathe the air. I also want to live. I know very well that if you don't, we don't, they don't, I can't. That's what it is all about. But we have to achieve some kind of vocabulary. I must say I think we've begun it. To tell you the truth, I think we've begun it—to translate for each other and then for many others. You, your experience, and me, my experience, because your experience does not matter as Margaret Mead and my experience doesn't matter as Jimmy Baldwin. What does matter is what we can do with it, not for you, not for me, but for all those people who don't know the discipline, the passion, the love. You know it goes into a vast amount of effort, and for what a vast amount of effort how little it can produce. You're talking about time and history and I am, too. It takes a long, long time, doesn't it?

MEAD: Yes.

BALDWIN: You don't belong to you any more than I belong to me.

MEAD: No.

BALDWIN: We're talking about that. I have to talk out of my beginnings, and I did begin here auctioned like a mule, bred as though I were a stallion. I was in my country, which I paid for and I'm paying for. Treated as not even a beast is treated. Died in ditches not even as a mule is murdered. And I have to remember that. I have to redeem that. I cannot let it go for nothing. The only reason I'm here is to bear witness.

I don't *really* like my life, you know. I don't really want another drink. I've seen enough of the world's cities to make me vomit forever. But I've got something to do. It has nothing in it any longer for me. What I wanted is what everybody wanted. You wanted it, too. Everybody wanted it. It will come. It comes in different shapes and forms. It is not despair, and the price one pays is everybody's price.

But on top of that particular price, which is universal, there is something gratuitous which I will not forgive, you know. It's difficult to be born, difficult to learn to walk, difficult to grow old, difficult to die and difficult to live for everybody, everywhere, forever. But no one has a right to put on top of that another burden, another price which nobody can pay, and a burden which really nobody can bear. I know it's universal, Margaret, but the fact that it is universal doesn't mean that I'll accept it.

MARGARET MEAD, renowned anthropologist and author, was Adjunct Professor of Anthropology at Columbia University. She was also Curator Emeritus of Ethnology at the American Museum of Natural History, where she created a new exhibition hall, Peoples of the Pacific. Dr. Mead's books include *Coming of Age in Samoa, Growing Up in New Guinea, Male and Female, New Lives for Old,* and *Culture and Commitment.*

JAMES BALDWIN established himself as one of the most important writers of the century with his novels, essays, and plays. Mr. Baldwin's books include *Nobody Knows My Name, The Fire Next Time, Another Country, Go Tell It on the Mountain,* and *No Name in the Street. Blues for Mister Charlie* has been produced on Broadway and throughout the world. He lived in Paris and Istanbul and traveled in Africa, England, and the United States.